The Cash and Carter

FAMILY COOKBOOK

The CASH and CARTER

FAMILY COOKBOOK

Recipes *and* Recollections *from* Johnny and June's Table

John Carter Cash

NELSON
BOOKS

An Imprint of Thomas Nelson

Published in Nashville, Tennessee, by Nelson Books, an imprint of Thomas Nelson. Nelson Books and Thomas Nelson are registered trademarks of HarperCollins Christian Publishing, Inc.

Interior food photography by Tambi Lane Photography.

Recipe testing/editing and food styling by Donna Britt.

Thomas Nelson titles may be purchased in bulk for educational, business, fund-raising, or sales promotional use. For information, please e-mail SpecialMarkets@ThomasNelson.com.

ISBN 978-1-4002-1262-0 (signed)
ISBN 978-1-4002-0189-1 (eBook)
ISBN 978-1-4002-0188-4 (HC)

Library of Congress Control Number: 2018941279

Printed in China

18 19 20 21 22   DSC   10 9 8 7 6 5 4 3 2 1

CONTENTS

This book is dedicated to my wife, Ana Cristina Cash. Without her, this book would not have been possible. Ana Cristina shares my love for fine cuisine, fun foods, cooking, and adventure. I also dedicate this to my daughter Grace June Cash, son Jack Ezra Cash, daughter Anna "AnnaBelle" Maybelle Cash, and my eldest son, Joseph John Cash.

A quick bite with my parents on the road in 1979.

Below: Mom in front of her dining table on the first floor of our home in Hendersonville.

1973. From left: George T. Kelly, Rosey's Friend, my sister Rosey Carter Nix, Dad, JCC, my mother, and Winafred "K" Kelly.

Introduction

Suppertime: Around the Cash and Carter Family Table

Come home, come home, it's suppertime,
the daylight's fading fast.
Come home, come home, it's suppertime,
We're going home at last . . .
—JOHN R CASH, "SUPPERTIME"

John R Cash

In the cotton fields of Arkansas, where my father grew up, life was hard. The Great Depression had hit the rural community of Kingsland hard, and when my dad was born toward the end of the winter, on February 23, 1932, his father, my grandfather Ray Cash, was seeking work.

My father's mother, Carrie Rivers Cash, did all she could to raise her children with love and dignity. Carrie's father was a pastor who tended not only to his own family's needs, but also to those of the community. Carrie, like her father, was tall, strong, and not afraid to get her hands dirty. She worked side by side with her husband and her children. It was a way of life. Through it all, there were two things that remained steadfast. One was the family's faith in God, the other was suppertime.

In 1936 my grandfather Ray, along with Carrie and his children, made ready to move to northeast Arkansas. Ray applied to be part of a government program called Dyess Colony, put in place by President Franklin Delano Roosevelt. Through the program, he was actually able to purchase, in his own name, twenty acres of the rich, black-soiled land for growing cotton. Ray loaded up his family and all their belongings into a mule-drawn carriage and headed to Pine Bluff, where he caught the train north to the Mississippi River Delta flatlands.

The family worked hard to plant and harvest their crops, and though life was physically challenging, the family clung to each other with love. In large part, their success or failure as farmers depended on the weather. If there wasn't enough rain during the growing season, the cotton harvest was smaller. If the summer was hot and dry, the crops would suffer.

Sometimes food was scarce. Dad told me that there were days when they had no beans, fatback pork, or cornmeal; the milk cow was dry; and they had no chickens for eggs. It was on days like this that my grandfather might turn to my father, hand him a single .22-caliber rifle shell, point to the gun, and say, "Go get me a rabbit." If Dad couldn't find

Ray and Carrie Cash.

Dad in shorts wearing Mom's apron.

a rabbit, or if he missed the one he fired at, the outcome was simple: they didn't eat.

But no matter the food upon the table, no time was more important than the daily gatherings at suppertime. Carrie was a wonderful cook. In the early days in Dyess and through much of World War II, they had no electricity in their home, so she made all her meals on a wood-burning stove. Even if there was meager fare, she fed her family the finest of all foods: those prepared with love. On a fall morning, halfway through the cotton harvest, the children might wake to find a hearty breakfast of salted pork belly, eggs, and buttermilk biscuits served with milk gravy. During the workweek, lunch was light, typically bread and peanut butter, perhaps with some homemade jam. Dinner was, more often than not, a heaping bowl of beans and cornbread. Dessert was simply more cornbread, crumbled into a glass of buttermilk—one of my father's all-time favorite snacks.

Sunday was a well-deserved day of rest for the Cash family, and the Sunday meals were hearty when the weather, harvest, and pocketbook allowed. Dinner would perhaps consist of fried chicken, slow-cooked green beans with ham hock, mashed potatoes with gravy, fried corn, and, on special occasions, one of Carrie's wondrous desserts, such as her delicious banana bread.

Here, I sit with my grandparents and their pet parrot outside their Tennessee home.

At the dining table my father knew as a child, he learned the value of the family coming close together. Suppertime meant the day had ended, the hard work was done, and it was time to gather, not only to dine, but to laugh, tell stories, and unite as a family before heading back into the fields the next day.

When Dad was only twelve, the family faced a terrible tragedy: his brother Jack died in a horrible accident. Jack had been a loving, intelligent, and deeply spiritual boy. Even at fourteen, he had planned to become a pastor, and his personal Bible still sits on my shelf, annotated in lead pencil marks. Dad never really got over Jack's death and was deeply inspired by his brother throughout his life to delve deeper into his own faith.

In early 1950, Dad turned eighteen, and after graduating high school, he left Dyess to join the air force. After serving three years as a high-speed Morse code interceptor in Germany, he was honorably discharged. When he came back to the United States, he married his first wife, Vivian, almost immediately. He tried his hand at various careers, but music was in his heart. It became his driving force.

In Scotland in 1981, with my father, preparing for a feast of fresh-caught trout.

He and Vivian had four daughters: Rosanne, Kathy, Cindy, and Tara. He loved them with all he had, though he struggled in many ways with his own internal demons, addictions, and sadness. The years of the mid-1960s were hard times for Dad, and he was home very little. He was thin and distanced, not only from the family at home who loved him, but from most everyone. He made some wonderful music through those years, but inside he was seeking peace and was perhaps his own worst enemy. In 1967, he hit a hard rock bottom with his addiction. Gratefully, there were those who helped him back up, supported him, and gave him strength. By 1967 he and Vivian had divorced. Though he had known and worked with June Carter for years, it wasn't until then that his love for my mother truly flourished.

Valerie June Carter

At the Foot of Clinch Mountain

My grandmother Maybelle Carter was the Queen of Country Music, and that's not just a proud grandson speaking. I remember my mother telling me this about my grandmother when I was young and not quite believing her. I didn't learn to appreciate "Mother" Maybelle's impact on the world until I was in my thirties. That's when I began to study the Carter Family's music and discovered that Mom was telling the truth. She wasn't alone in her belief—far from it. A good many history books agree.

Maybelle Carter was creator of a guitar style commonly known as "The Carter Scratch." This style was developed essentially out of necessity, since she was both the rhythm and lead player most of the time in her family band. She weaved together bass string melody lines, chord strums, and high string rhythms to create a sound no one had ever heard before. She played ornate guitar parts on her Gibson L-5 archtop acoustic. Her style directly influenced artists such as Chet Atkins, Doc Watson, Bill Monroe, Jerry Garcia, Joan Baez, Bob Dylan, and Keith Richards—and thousands of others list these musicians as their own direct influence. Maybelle was the foundation of so much, particularly what we now know as acoustic and electric guitar playing in country, blues, or rock. I would go so far as to say there is something of Maybelle's influence in each and every note you may hear of music recorded between 1941 and today.

The Carter Family not only recorded more than three hundred songs in their careers from 1927 to 1941, but also spread country music

My mother, June, performing, seated and playing the banjo with (standing, from the left) my grandmother Maybelle Carter and my aunts Helen and Anita Carter.

to the world through border radio stations. These stations, just across the Mexican border, were broadcasting a staggering 500,000 watts of signal. In the United States, then as it is now, the limit was 100,000 watts. The Mexican laws were different in those days, and these stations broadcast a signal so powerful it could be picked up for thousands of miles. Beginning in the late 1930s and early 1940s, people all over the Western Hemisphere were listening to the Carter Family's "hillbilly music," as it was called then.

By the time she was ten years old, my mother, June, was performing with her family, and she remembered those border stations.

"The signal was so powerful," she told me, "that you could lie quietly in bed at night and listen to the radio through your dental fillings!"

As a boy, I recall visiting my grandmother and spending time with her. She made homemade pickles, and I remember helping her make them as young as five years old. She worked her whole life as a performing musician, but there was nothing more important to her than togetherness of family, and there was no better place to keep that family close than at the supper table.

Cooking was a close-knit Carter Family tradition, and the very nature of Maybelle's country life meant she was surrounded by good, fresh ingredients. She grew up in southwestern Virginia, at the base of a great limestone outcropping called Clinch Mountain. Her home was in Maces Spring, and though that land was referred to by the locals as "Poor Valley" because of the low quality of soil in the area, everyone still had their own gardens and fruit orchards and raised their own pigs and cattle for slaughter.

My grandmother served a bountiful harvest of summer vegetables when

My grandparents Ezra and Maybelle Carter in the 1960s, with a truck full of huge redfish, Port Richey, Florida.

My thirteenth birthday party with Dad,
my sister Cindy, and Mom.

available, but the vast majority of tomatoes, squash, okra, and beans were canned and stored underground in a basement cellar. Each farm up and down the valley had its own smokehouse, and a pig was slaughtered in the winter, and the hams cured through the colder months. As spring warmed things up, the hams were smoked. Today's store-bought country hams are nothing like the ones I ate in Virginia as a boy. For one thing, they weren't quite as salty. My cousins, who knew the methods, finished the curing and smoking by sealing the hams in brown sugar and honey, offering a sweet softness to cut the salty ham.

These days, farm-fresh tomatoes are often hard to come by, unless you grow them yourself. If you really want to taste what a tomato tasted like all those years ago, you would need to find some heirloom seeds. I guarantee that anyone who has tasted a vine-ripened tomato, from old seed, grown in their own garden, knows the difference. The first time someone tastes one they usually say, "Oh! So that is what a tomato really tastes like!" I have witnessed this numerous times.

Because of their musical talents, the Carter Family traveled the world, and while doing so, my mother expanded her culinary knowledge, tasting foods and flavors she never would have found in her Clinch Mountain home. She developed epicurean tastes, learning to cook many of the dishes she encountered, adding her own creativity and flair to each creation.

With my grandmother Maybelle, 1975 or '76.

Through it all, she never gave up her simple nature and never forgot where she came from. She was a poor valley girl, with a richness of heart that she shared with all she met. When she gathered family and friends around her table—no matter if it was Paul McCartney, Charlie Pride, Prince Charles, or an elderly neighbor—she treated them the same. She fed them the same fare and used the same silverware, crystal, and place settings.

June loved strongly, purely, and openly, never turning from her upbringing, and her table was a gathering place where she brought those in her life closer into her own fold.

Johnny Cash and June Carter Cash

My Mother and Father, Our Life in Tennessee and on the Road

My parents met backstage at the Ryman Auditorium one night during a performance of the *Grand Ole Opry* in 1956. The legend is (and we can believe it or not—they were the only two there) that my father walked up to my mom and in that deep and powerful voice of his said, "Hello, I'm Johnny Cash, and I'm going to marry you someday." Supposedly my mother answered back with her unique and quick wit, "I can't wait!" while pointing at the wedding ring on her left hand. (She was married to country singer Carl Smith at the time.) Whether this is the exact history, we may never know, but I believe it. This sounds like them, on both sides. It would prove to be quite a foretelling.

In 1967, after my father had turned his life around, given up the

Wedding reception, March 1, 1968, at the home by the lake, Hendersonville, TN.

amphetamines that had ruled his life, and reestablished his relationship with God, he recorded "Jackson," a song with June Carter that would end up being a Grammy-winning hit. Then, in February 1968, live on stage at the Ryman Auditorium, Dad and Mom announced to the world they were to be wed. They married the next day, March 1, 1968, in a small chapel in Franklin, Kentucky.

They moved into the home my father had already bought in Hendersonville, Tennessee. Back then, Hendersonville was a tiny town, and the lakeside home where they lived was unlike any other place on earth. It was built by a unique-minded builder named Braxton Dixon, who not only had vision like no other but was able to use the local stone and wood to fashion a home

Top: The Highwaymen with a friend. From left: Kris Kristofferson, Dad, Willie Nelson, Hank Williams Jr., and Waylon Jennings.

Photo by Billy Mitchell (www.BillyMitchell.com)

Middle: Waylon, Mom, and Jessi Colter in Bon Aqua, Tennessee, mid-1970s.

Photo by John R Cash

Bottom: A card game with the beloved Jessi Colter on the back porch of my parents' home in Jamaica, "Cinnamon Hill."

Photo by John R Cash

against the cliffside, right next to Old Hickory Lake, through which ran the Cumberland River on its way to Nashville.

My mother had two daughters, Carlene and Rosie, who moved in with them, and within two years, my mom and dad had added on two more stories to the home. The ceiling of their master bedroom was an arched vault of over twenty-six feet.

They tried for a while to have a child but were unsuccessful. Then, almost two years to the day from their wedding, on March 3, 1970, I was born at a hospital just down the road in Madison, Tennessee.

At that time, my parents were at the very apex of their careers. Dad had a live television show, *The Johnny Cash Show*, being broadcast around the Western Hemisphere.

Gathered around the lakeside room at the Cash Family home, 1990. From left: Tom T. Hall, Skeeter Davis, Bobby Bare, Mom, Anita Carter, Dad, Helen Carter, Diana Christiansen, Earl Scruggs, Bill Monroe, family friend (man with grey hair in the back), my first cousin Rhonda Ponessa, Mark Collie, and Rodney Crowell.

© Photograph by Alan MESSER | www.alanmesser.com

I was only a three-month-old babe when they brought me out on stage and presented me to the world.

So my travels began as an infant on the road with my parents, and I traveled extensively with them for the next twenty-seven years. In April 1970, Mom and Dad brought me to the White House by invitation from then-president Richard Nixon. The president had asked Dad to perform some songs, and while Dad sang, I was put down for a nap in the Lincoln bed. By the time I was three months old I had traveled to Germany and the United Kingdom. By eleven months I had been to Israel and Australia. By the time I was ten I had been to forty-nine states and soon after made it to my fiftieth—strangely enough, it was Mississippi, even though it borders Tennessee. Dad just hadn't performed any shows in Mississippi up to that point.

I typically went to Europe (Germany and the United Kingdom) twice a year and usually at least once a year to Australia. Dad was well known in all these places, and I was always a part of his show. When I was old enough to walk, my parents would bring me onstage and let me take a bow for the crowd. When I could follow the melody, I sang the Carter Family songs and gospel songs at the end of the show.

Though my parents didn't push me to be in the music business, I was destined by the love I developed for music. This is what

Top: Mom's table set for a party.

My mother in the 1990s, her fine linens set, her home decorated and adorned, and a delicious assortment of foods, ready to eat.

my parents taught me: do what you love. I do what I love, and I have found my place in the recording studio. Though my first records were done working for my parents, I have been recording Loretta Lynn for the past eleven years, having coproduced with her daughter Patsy more than a hundred songs. I have produced thousands of songs for various artists in my studio, The Cash Cabin, and it is here I do what I can to carry on my parents' musical heritage, following what I love and making music I believe in with artists of integrity and high talent.

On my parents' music tours I discovered my love for good food, and I must give my mother the large part of the credit. She took me to fine restaurants and taught me to appreciate the culinary experiences, the preparation and presentation along with the tastes.

Back home, we ate a great deal of Southern food, thanks in part to our marvelous cook Ms. Letha. Traditional Southern food was often our daily fare, but not always, as you will find in the coming pages. I learned to cook from Ms. Letha, my mother, other ladies who worked at the house, and from chefs around the world.

My natural love for the Southern food of my homeland was intertwined with the tastes of the world, from Indonesian to Cajun, from kosher deli sandwiches to Argentinian churrasco. Nothing was off the menu, and nothing was bizarre to me. It was all just good food. It was that love for good food that guided and inspired me then, and it still does now.

This love for foods of the world is something I have shared with my children. At the time of this writing, Joseph is twenty-two, AnnaBelle is seventeen, Jack is twelve, and Grace is five months old. The elder three have grown up in a household where a typical breakfast of biscuits and gravy may be followed by a lunch of mixed French greens with salmon from the Faroe Islands and a dinner of flash-fried sweetbreads with yellow beets or Jamaican venison burgers. Nothing surprises them. It is the nature of our lives.

Through the years I have continued to cook my old favorite recipes, those of my family's, those I learned in my travels, and those of my own creation. I'm sharing many of them with you in this collection. My wife, Ana Cristina, and my children are also creative cooks, and some of their favorite recipes will also be found in this book. No matter the food on the table, no matter the cook or the setting, whether served on my mother's fine china with silver or on paper plates with paper napkins, one thing has not changed since those days of my father's youth in Arkansas and my mother's in Virginia. At the table, family is brought close, love is within the heart of the table, and we are all drawn together there, closer than any other place in the home.

Note from John Carter Cash

I am pleased to let you know that each cake, main course, appetizer, and so on, for which you see a photo, was homemade, using the exact recipes in this book. The dishes—the glassware, silverware, plates, saucers, and bowls—you see in the photographs are Ana Cristina's and my personal china and family heirlooms, including several different patterns of my mother's china. Included are cast-iron pots and pans that were in daily use at my parents' home for years. I now use them every day in my own home. The photos were taken on location, on my mom and dad's huge, mahogany dining-room table (now in my home) and at the Cash Cabin Studio, which my dad built in 1979 as a private refuge for himself and his family. Originally a one-room log cabin, this historical location has evolved over the years into a state-of-the-art recording studio. My father and mother recorded there later in life, and since then it has been an operative recording studio, where dozens of artists and musicians regularly make music. The pictures themselves resonate within these pages with authenticity and history, reflecting the genuine love and spirit of the stories and recipes in this collection.

CHAPTER 1

Early to Rise, Happy, Healthy, and Wise–Breakfast at the Cash Home

June's Homemade Southern-Style Biscuits

One of the main traditional ingredients for Southern biscuits is self-rising flour, something that is not always readily available outside of the South. For those who can't find the premade mix of bleached white flour, baking powder, baking soda, and salt, this version of my mother's biscuit recipe uses regular, easy to find, all-purpose white flour. When making homemade Southern biscuits, there are a few steps that need to be carefully followed.

3 tablespoons shortening, plus
    more for biscuit preparation
    and for greasing the pan
2 cups all-purpose flour, plus
    more for dusting

1 tablespoon baking powder
3/4 teaspoon baking soda
1 teaspoon salt
1 tablespoon melted butter
1 cup cold buttermilk

Preheat the oven to 425 degrees. Grease a nonstick rimmed 8 x 11 or 9 x 13 baking sheet with a generous portion of shortening and set aside.

In a large bowl combine the flour, baking powder, baking soda, and salt. Sift this mixture into another large bowl. Add 3 tablespoons of the shortening and the melted butter to the flour mixture, and use your fingers or a pastry cutter to evenly combine.

Make a well in the flour mixture, and pour in a little of the buttermilk. Use a fork or rubber spatula to stir a small portion of the flour mixture into the buttermilk. Continue to pour the buttermilk in a little at a time, pulling more flour from the edges of the bowl until the dough is well mixed.

Dust a large cutting board and a rolling pin with flour. Sprinkle a little more flour on top of the dough, leaving some on your hands, and then form the dough into a large ball. Place the dough on the cutting board, and roll it to a thickness of 1/2 inch. Rub a light layer of shortening on half of the rolled-out dough, and then fold the dough in half. Roll the dough out again. Rub some shortening on half of the dough, fold over, and roll out again. Repeat rubbing with shortening and folding and rolling out two more times. Use a 3-inch biscuit or cookie cutter to cut out the biscuits. Place the biscuits upside down, slightly apart on the baking sheet, and coat them with the shortening. Then turn them over. You'll now have a bit of shortening on the top of the biscuits as well, which is what you want. Gather the dough scraps, and roll the dough again, cutting as many biscuits as possible.

Place the baking sheet in the oven, and bake until the biscuits are tall and the tops are golden brown, about 20 minutes. Remove the biscuits from the oven and serve immediately.

Makes 10 (3-inch) biscuits.

JOHN CARTER'S TIP: You can easily make buttermilk by adding 1 tablespoon of white vinegar to 1 cup of milk. Let stand for 5 minutes, and then stir.

Mother Maybelle Carter's Tomato Gravy

When I traveled to southwestern Virginia as a boy with my parents, I noticed that my mother seemed to step back in time while we were visiting her home. Particularly when she was near her first cousin Fern, my mother could really be herself. I sensed that, in her heart, she had returned to the simple strength of her humble roots, and the regal and refined lady who may have visited the White House a week before took second seat to "Little Junie Carter."

I have always felt that when we grow up with someone, some strong bonds are created through joy. During those mornings at the foot of Clinch Mountain, laughter and camaraderie would accompany the wondrous food set on the table. Both my grandmother and grandfather were cooks, and their garden was full every summer. Grandmother Maybelle canned her own tomatoes after the harvest and used them for a number of her dishes, including this one. Biscuits and gravy is a Southern breakfast staple, but this variation is unique to the region of Virginia that my family is from, and as far as I know, you won't find it anywhere else in the country.

4 ounces Southern-style breakfast
    sausage, chopped into chunks
⅓ cup all-purpose flour
2 cups milk

1 cup canned diced tomatoes with juices,
    store-bought or home-canned
¼ cup pure cane sugar or white sugar
Salt and black pepper to taste

Place the sausage in a large skillet, and fry over medium heat until golden brown. Be careful not to get the pan too hot as the sausage may burn. Once browned, leave the sausage and rendered grease in the pan. Reduce the heat to medium-low, and slowly add the flour, stirring constantly. Cook the flour in the sausage and grease mixture until it becomes golden, 6 or 7 minutes. Keep an eye on the grease and make sure it doesn't get too hot. Increase the heat to medium-high, and stir in the milk. Stir constantly until the gravy begins to thicken. Add the tomatoes and sugar, and continue stirring until the gravy returns to a boil. Immediately remove from the heat. Add salt and black pepper. Serve with June's Homemade Southern-Style Biscuits.

Makes 1 ½ to 2 cups.

Cash Family Easy Hash Brown Casserole

Hash brown casserole wasn't cooked often at my home, but when we were visiting my family in Virginia, my mother would make it special for my cousin Joe Carter, who loved it. Joe, the second child of Sara and A. P. Carter, had a great love for music, food, and family. I remember him sitting outside the door on the front porch of the Virginia home, my mother cooking at the stove, and Joe sticking his head in the door to ask, "Hash browns done yet, June? Sure smells good!"

In this recipe, frozen hash brown potatoes may be used, but shredding the potatoes is fairly easy, and to me, it makes a sizable difference. If using frozen potatoes, let them thaw overnight in the fridge, and then drain off any excess liquid.

Cooking spray

3 large baking potatoes, unpeeled, shredded, and moisture squeezed out to equal 20 ounces or 2 1/2 cups

1 1/2 cups shredded Cheddar cheese (Mom and Dad both preferred extra-sharp, but use medium if you prefer.)

1/4 cup diced onions

1 garlic clove, crushed

1 (10 1/2-ounce) can cream of chicken soup

1/4 teaspoon cayenne pepper, optional

Salt and black pepper

1/4 cup (1/2 stick) unsalted butter

Preheat the oven to 375 degrees. Coat a 2-quart casserole dish with cooking spray.

In a large bowl combine the shredded potatoes, cheese, onions, garlic, soup, and cayenne pepper, if using. Add salt and black pepper. (Most canned soups already have loads of salt in them, so keep that in mind when you add more salt.) Cut the butter into 4 even tablespoons. Press each pat of butter into the bottom of the casserole dish at even intervals. Cover the butter pats with the potato mixture. Cover the dish with foil, and bake for 30 to 40 minutes. Remove the foil, and increase the oven temperature to 400 degrees. Cook an additional 5 to 10 minutes, until the top is golden brown. Remove from the oven, and let sit for at least 10 minutes before serving.

Makes 4 to 6 servings.

JOHN CARTER'S TIP: You can use whatever kind of potatoes you want for this casserole, but russet or yellow potatoes, like Yukon Gold, are good choices. The key is to squeeze out as much moisture as you can before mixing the shredded potatoes with the other ingredients.

Jack Ezra Cash's Scotch Eggs

I first remember having Scotch eggs in Edinburgh when I was a boy. It is a delicious, single-package meal with sausage, a boiled egg, and bread crumbs—a full breakfast in a few bites. My son Jack went to Scotland with me when he was seven and never forgot his first Scotch eggs. They made such an impact on him that when we got home, he had to make some. Even at twelve, he's an accomplished cook, and this, his favorite breakfast, is one of his specialties. I love spending time with my son in the kitchen, and I'm there to offer a helping hand, especially when hot oil is involved.

I recommend a nice dash of hot sauce on top of the eggs, although on travels to the United Kingdom, I have found them served often with hot mustard.

1 quart water, plus more for a bowl of ice
9 large eggs, divided
2 cups ice
2 tablespoons milk
½ cup (or more) all-purpose flour

1 cup (or more) fine dried bread crumbs
1 pound Southern-style breakfast sausage
3 cups vegetable or peanut
 oil, for deep frying
Salt and black pepper to taste

Pour the water into a 4-quart saucepan, and bring to a boil over medium-high heat. Using a large spoon, lower 6 of the eggs into the boiling water one at a time. Boil the eggs for 10 minutes.

While the eggs boil, place 2 cups of ice in a large bowl, and add enough water to cover the ice. At the end of the boiling time, carefully pour the boiling water into the sink, and place the eggs in the ice-water bath for 5 minutes. Remove the eggs, and peel immediately.

Crack the remaining 3 eggs into a medium bowl, add the milk, and beat until combined. Pour the flour into a small bowl and the bread crumbs into another small bowl. Divide the sausage into 6 equal portions, and pat out each portion to roughly the size of the palm of your hand, being careful to make it about ⅛ inch thick. Wrap each sausage portion around a boiled egg, completely covering it.

Roll one sausage-covered egg lightly in the flour, place it in the beaten-egg mixture to coat, and roll it in the bread crumbs. Dip it into the egg mixture once more, and roll in the bread crumbs again. Repeat with the remaining 5 eggs. You may refrigerate the breaded eggs at this time if you're not ready to fry them right away.

Pour the oil into a deep pot or deep fryer, being careful not to fill it more than halfway.

Heat the oil over medium-high heat, until it sizzles when a bread crumb is dropped in. Use a large spoon to lower each breaded egg into the oil, being careful not to overcrowd the pot. You may have to cook the eggs in batches.

Fry until golden brown, for about 12 minutes. Remove the eggs to a plate or platter, and sprinkle lightly with salt and pepper.

Slice each egg in half, and serve immediately. Be careful. They will be very hot.

Makes 6 servings.

JOHN CARTER'S TIP: This is a deep-fried item. Use caution!

Cheesy Egg and Hot Dog Scramble

This simple dish was a regular favorite around our table when I was growing up. My mother and Nanny "K" made it regularly. "K" was the nanny my parents hired to watch after me while they traveled. (Her name was Winafred Kelly, but "K" was short for her last name; it was easier for me to say.) My dad particularly enjoyed this dish and would often add a single slice of American cheese to the top.

1 teaspoon vegetable oil
4 hot dogs, sliced into small pieces
8 large eggs

Salt and black pepper
6 ounces shredded Cheddar cheese, mild or
   sharp

Heat the vegetable oil in a nonstick skillet over medium heat. Add the hot dog pieces, and cook until brown. Crack the eggs into a small bowl, and beat them with a fork. Add salt and black pepper. Pour the eggs over the hot dog pieces, stirring and scrambling the eggs until light and fluffy. Sprinkle the cheese over the egg and hot dog mixture, and remove the pan from the heat. Serve immediately with biscuits or your favorite toasted bread.

Makes 4 servings.

Uncle Tube's Cheese Grits

The Carters were kind and gentle people, and none more so than Uncle Tube. Tube was my grandmother Maybelle's brother, and he was around a lot when I was a child. His wife, Babe, was quite a cook. I remember once visiting them in Hiltons, Virginia. I showed up at eight o'clock in the morning unannounced, but Babe already had breakfast on the table as if she knew I was coming (and these were the days before cell phones). I recall these cheesy grits that were still hot when I sat down. They were so good I ate more than I likely should have!

Vegetable oil for greasing the pan
2 cups water
1 tablespoon butter
1 teaspoon salt
1/2 teaspoon black pepper
2 1/2 cups quick 5-minute grits

2 cups shredded mild Cheddar cheese
4 large eggs
3 cups whole milk
1 garlic clove, minced
1/4 teaspoon paprika
1/4 teaspoon cayenne pepper, or to taste

Preheat the oven to 325 degrees. Grease a 9 x 13-inch baking dish with vegetable oil.

Place the water and butter in a large saucepan, and bring to a boil over high heat. Add the salt and black pepper, and then slowly whisk in the grits. Continue to whisk while the grits boil until there are no lumps, for 1 to 2 minutes. Reduce the heat to medium-low, and simmer the grits for 5 minutes.

Remove the pot from the heat. Add the cheese to the grits, and stir well.

Crack the eggs into a large bowl, and beat them well with a fork. Add the milk, garlic, paprika, and cayenne pepper. Stir to combine. Slowly pour the milk mixture into the grits, and mix well. Spoon the mixture into the baking dish. Bake uncovered for 50 to 60 minutes, until the mixture is set. Remove the pan from the oven, and allow the grits to stand for 5 minutes before serving.

Makes 6 to 8 servings.

Irish-Style Steel-Cut Oats with Buttermilk

2 1/2 cups water

1 tablespoon butter, plus more for serving

1 cup steel-cut oats

1 cup whole milk, divided

1/2 cup whole buttermilk, plus
   more for serving

Pinch of salt

1 tablespoon brown sugar

Pour the water into a medium saucepan, cover, and bring to a boil over high heat.

Melt the butter in another medium saucepan over medium heat. Add the oats, and cook until they begin to brown, 1 to 2 minutes. Pour the boiling water over the oats, and bring the mixture to a boil. Reduce the heat to medium-low, and simmer the oats uncovered for 15 minutes, stirring only occasionally. Add 1/2 cup of the whole milk, and simmer for an additional 10 minutes or until milk is absorbed.

Combine the remaining 1/2 cup of milk with the buttermilk in a small bowl. Pour the milk mixture over the oats. Add a pinch of salt. Cook for 10 to 12 minutes more or until desired thickness. Serve in a bowl with a small dab of butter, a sprinkling of brown sugar, and a dash of buttermilk.

Makes 4 servings.

Cheddar Cheese and Southern-Style Sausage Frittata

1 pound Southern-style breakfast sausage

1 (16-ounce) package frozen
   shredded hash browns

Salt and black pepper to taste

3 tablespoons salted butter

6 slices brioche or sourdough bread

8 to 9 large eggs, beaten well

1 (16-ounce) package shredded mild
   Cheddar cheese

Preheat the oven to 375 degrees.

Place the sausage in a medium skillet, and cook over medium heat, using a large spoon to crumble the sausage, until browned. Transfer the sausage to a large bowl. Place the hash browns in the same skillet, and cook, stirring constantly over medium heat, until the potatoes begin to wilt, 4 to 6 minutes. Add the salt and black pepper to taste. Add the hash browns to the sausage, and stir until combined.

Cut the butter into 6 pieces, and place them evenly in the bottom of a 9 x 13-inch or 2 1/2- to 3-quart baking dish. Place the slices of bread over the pats of butter, covering the bottom of the dish. Pour the eggs over the bread. Spread the sausage and hash brown mixture over the eggs.

Cover the pan with foil. Place the pan in the oven, and bake for 10 minutes. Remove the pan from the oven, remove the foil, and top the frittata with the cheese. Return the pan to the oven, and bake, uncovered, for 7 minutes, or until cheese is completely melted and beginning to brown. Remove the pan from the oven, and let stand for 10 minutes before serving.

Makes 4 to 6 servings.

Homemade Pancakes with Fresh Berry Compote

This Fresh Berry Compote is easy to make and tastes delicious with pancakes. My mother also served it with her Heavenly Hash and Cheesecake (recipes in chapter 6).

Fresh Berry Compote

4 tablespoons salted butter

1 cup sliced strawberries

1 cup blueberries

1 cup blackberries

2 cups pure cane sugar or white sugar

Pinch of salt

2 tablespoons cornstarch

1/2 cup cold water

Pancakes

2 cups all-purpose flour

1 tablespoon baking powder

1/4 teaspoon salt

1 large egg

1 1/2 cups milk (a bit more if you prefer thinner batter)

1/4 cup half-and-half

1 teaspoon vanilla extract

1/2 cup (1 stick) butter, plus more for serving

1/4 cup powdered sugar

Whipped cream

To prepare the compote, place the butter in a large saucepan, and melt over medium-high heat. Stir in the berries, sugar, and salt, and bring to a boil. Reduce the heat to low, and cook the berries, covered, for 30 minutes, stirring occasionally.

In a small bowl whisk the cornstarch into the cold water until well mixed and smooth.

Increase the heat to medium, and return the berry mixture to a boil, stirring constantly. Add the cornstarch mixture to the berries. Continue to boil, stirring constantly, until the compote begins to thicken. Remove from the heat. Let the compote cool to room temperature before serving. Leftovers can be stored in the refrigerator for up to a week.

To prepare the pancakes, sift the flour into a large bowl. Add the baking powder and salt, and whisk to combine. Whisk in the egg, milk, half-and-half, and vanilla.

Heat a large nonstick skillet over medium heat, and add 2 tablespoons of the butter. When melted, spread the butter evenly in the pan.

Spoon the batter into the hot butter, using approximately ¼ cup of batter per pancake. Cook the pancakes until browned, about 3 minutes on each side. Remove the pancakes to a paper towel–lined plate. Cover with another paper towel to keep them warm while cooking the next batch of pancakes. Add more butter to the pan as needed for the remaining batches.

When all the pancakes are done, place them on a large platter, cover with the compote, sprinkle with the powdered sugar, and dollop on the whipped cream. Serve with more butter while still hot.

Makes 4 cups of compote and 18 (4-inch) pancakes.

Johnny's Sausage Gravy

Biscuits and gravy were at least a biweekly meal at my home growing up. I have eaten gravy all around the country, and it seems to me that Southern gravy has been misinterpreted by cooks north of the Mason-Dixon Line and by most culinary institutions. Most gravy, I've found, is more like a sausage cream sauce, while the gravy I grew up with is quite different from that. Gravy isn't hard to make, but like many other from-scratch basics, it takes practice to get it right. Trial and error will be your best friend in developing your own sausage gravy. This is an art, and each person may do gravy a bit differently. Take your time and experiment. It very well may turn out a bit different every time, and that's okay!

1 pound Southern-style breakfast sausage
1 tablespoon or more vegetable
   oil, if necessary

2 tablespoons all-purpose flour
1 cup milk
Salt and black pepper, optional

Pat out the sausage into small patties, reserving 2 or 3 ounces to crumble into the pan. Place the patties in a medium nonstick skillet, leaving an open space in the middle of the pan. Place the crumbled sausage in the open space you left in the middle of the pan. Fry the sausage over medium heat, until the patties are well done and dark brown on both sides. Remove all but the sausage crumbles from the pan, and place on paper towels to drain. Save the sausage patties to serve with your breakfast.

Check the grease in the skillet. The amount of grease will determine how much flour you will use. (I often have wild boar sausage, which has little fat, but most pork sausage has a lot of fat.) The bottom of the pan should be covered in a thin layer of grease. If there isn't much grease in the pan, add a little vegetable oil. Add in just enough flour to make a bubbling thin paste (about 2 tablespoons). The mixture should not be too thick.

Brown the flour over medium heat for several minutes, stirring constantly, making sure not to burn your sausage bits, flour, or grease.

Increase the heat to medium-high, and slowly pour in the milk, stirring constantly until the mixture is at a full boil. Decrease the heat if necessary to make sure the milk does not burn. Continue to stir until the gravy is thickened. Remove the gravy immediately from the heat. Add salt and pepper, if using, and serve hot with biscuits.

Makes 1 to 1 1/4 cups gravy.

Fried Bologna and Eggs with Biscuits and Fresh Tomatoes

Fried bologna was one of my father's favorite breakfasts. I remember smelling the aroma of it frying in the farm kitchen as I walked outside on winter days in Bon Aqua, Tennessee.

Dad would buy canned biscuits, eggs, and sliced bologna. He liked the bologna slices nearly crispy—some almost burned. He always loved crispy and well-done foods. While the canned biscuits were baking in the oven, he would scramble the eggs in the same skillet he had fried the bologna in. He never beat the eggs before putting them in the skillet to cook and simply half scrambled them in the bologna drippings, adding a copious amount of black pepper and a little salt. He piled two biscuits on a plate with the eggs and bologna. There was ketchup for the eggs and bologna, and local honey and butter for the biscuits. Simple, but very much one of his favorite foods. I loved it then and still love it now.

1 (16-ounce) can refrigerated biscuits
1 1/2 teaspoons vegetable oil
6 slices bologna
6 large eggs

Salt and black pepper to taste
2 to 3 fresh tomatoes, sliced
Butter
Local raw or regular honey

Preheat the oven to 350 degrees.

Place the biscuits on an ungreased cookie sheet. Place the sheet in the oven, and bake the biscuits for 12 to 16 minutes until golden brown on top.

While the biscuits bake, cut small slits into the edges of the bologna slices to keep them from curling up while frying. Heat the vegetable oil in a large nonstick skillet over medium heat. Add the bologna slices, and fry until crispy and browned. Remove the bologna to a paper towel–lined plate to drain.

Crack the eggs into the same skillet. Stir with a whisk, and cook over medium heat until the eggs are softly scrambled. If you prefer, you may fry your eggs. Add the salt and black pepper to taste.

Place the biscuits on a plate, add the bologna and eggs, and serve with the tomatoes, butter, and honey.

Makes 3 servings.

Raw Honey Drizzle Fruit Salad

Some people collect stamps, baseball cards, or fine wine, but I collect honey. Raw, uncontaminated honey lasts forever, and if it crystalizes, you can just melt it down and it's the same as it was. Having traveled extensively, I discovered that the honey in England was much different from the honey in north Florida. I have my favorites—Tupelo honey, Acacia, English Heather, Hawaiian White, Jamaican (I've never found it to be available outside of Jamaica, but if you visit Jamaica, I suggest giving it a try). I personally feel the best is local honey from your area, specifically from the hives within a 75-mile radius of your home. I had chronic allergies for years and began eating local honey as I had heard it helped. It took eating it daily for two and a half years, but I am now 90 percent cured of all pollen allergies.

2 medium bananas, thinly sliced
1 cup green seedless grapes, sliced in halves
1 apple, peeled and cut into small pieces
1 cup blueberries
1 cup strawberries, thinly sliced

1 cup small marshmallows
1/2 cup sugar
1/2 teaspoon vanilla extract
2 tablespoons raw or regular honey
Whipped cream, optional

Combine the bananas, grapes, apple, blueberries, and strawberries in a large bowl. Add the marshmallows, sugar, and vanilla, and gently stir. Refrigerate for at least 2 hours before serving. Drizzle with honey before serving. Top each serving with whipped cream, if using.

Makes 4 servings.

CHAPTER 2

Come Right In and Gather Round—Salads, Appetizers, Pickles, Sauces, and Marinades

In our home growing up, there was a world of flavors and enticing aromas drifting through the house on any given day, a wondrous array of scents of varied origins and ingredients from all over the globe. Yes, my parents were from the South, and many traditional Southern dishes were on the table daily. But there was also likely to be something from a recipe found in a French cookbook or perhaps a dish that my mom's friend from Israel had taught her to cook when we visited there.

The scent of freshly made Italian tomato sauce with oregano for homemade pizza just as quickly comes to my mind as the smell of fried chicken when I go back in time to my childhood. Here is a selection from my memories—truly foods of the world.

Homemade Mango and Cilantro Salsa

1/2 cup diced mango, ripe but still firm

1 cup diced Roma tomatoes
   (about 2 tomatoes)

1/2 cup diced sweet onions (like Walla
   Walla, Vidalia, or Texas Sweet)

3 tablespoons finely chopped garlic

2 tablespoons brown sugar (or less
   if you want it less sweet)

3 tablespoons chopped cilantro

1/4 cup diced jalapeño peppers, optional

Juice of 1/2 lemon

Juice of 1/2 lime

Salt and black pepper to taste

Place the mango, tomato, onions, garlic, brown sugar, cilantro, and jalapeños in a large bowl, and stir well. Pour the lemon and lime juices on top, and toss to combine well. Add the salt and black pepper to taste. Serve with corn chips, and store any leftovers in the refrigerator. The salsa will last several days in the refrigerator, depending on the freshness of your ingredients.

Makes 1 1/2 to 2 cups.

JOHN CARTER'S TIP: If mango is too ripe it will be hard to cut up, so choose a firm but ripe mango.

Marinated Cucumbers and Onions with Dill

2 pounds sliced garden or English
   cucumbers, peeled or not
   peeled (your preference)
1 large sweet onion (like Walla
   Walla, Vidalia, or Texas Sweet),
   sliced into thin strips
1/2 cup white vinegar

1/2 cup water, plus more to refill
2 tablespoons kosher salt
1 large sprig fresh dill, torn into
   pieces (about 2 tablespoons)
2 to 4 tablespoons pure cane or white sugar
Salt and black pepper to taste

Place the cucumbers and onions in a large bowl with a lid. Add the vinegar, water, salt, dill, and sugar. Add the salt and black pepper to taste. Cover and place in the refrigerator for at least 2 hours. Pour off about half of the briny liquid, and then refill the bowl with fresh water. Shake the vegetables around a bit. Chill a little longer. Stir well, and drain off most of the liquid before serving. The vegetables will keep in the refrigerator for a couple of weeks.

Makes about 6 servings.

Blue Cheese Pink Coleslaw

My mother made this tasty coleslaw with either blue or feta cheese. She and I always preferred the blue cheese version, though you may choose feta if you don't like the strong taste of the blue. I remember this coleslaw being served mostly in the summer, and its taste still reminds me of those summer afternoons traveling the United States on a tour bus. Mom had a full kitchen on the bus, and the many tastes of home never ceased.

Use a food processor to chop the beet, onion, and celery and to shred the carrots, or cut them by hand. To shred the cabbage, cut it into quarters, stand each piece on its side, and remove the core. Using a sharp knife, slice the cabbage pieces until shredded.

1 small raw beet, peeled and chopped
3 medium carrots, shredded
1/2 cup finely chopped sweet onion (like Walla Walla, Vidalia, or Texas Sweet)
5 celery ribs, finely diced
1/2 head red cabbage, shredded

1/4 cup cider vinegar
3/4 cup crumbled blue or feta cheese
1 cup mayonnaise
Salt and black pepper to taste
3 pieces crisply fried bacon, crumbled

Place the beets, carrots, onion, celery, and cabbage in a large bowl.

In a separate bowl stir together the vinegar, blue cheese, and mayonnaise. Add the salt and black pepper to taste. Stir the cheese mixture into the vegetables. Add the bacon, and stir again. Refrigerate for at least 2 hours or overnight before serving.

Makes about 6 cups.

Baby Arugula and Raspberry Summer Salad with Homemade Vinaigrette Dressing

This salad is one I make regularly around my home and is one of my wife Ana Cristina's and my very favorite salads.

Vinaigrette Dressing

1 cup red wine vinegar

1/2 cup extra-virgin olive oil

2 tablespoons pure cane
    sugar or white sugar

1 1/2 teaspoons dried oregano

1 1/2 teaspoons garlic powder

1 1/2 teaspoons salt

1 1/2 teaspoons black pepper

Salad

1 large package of baby arugula,
    about 5 ounces

1 cup shredded carrots

1/2 cup raspberries

1/4 cup chopped walnuts

1/2 cup crumbled feta cheese

To prepare the dressing, in a small bowl whisk together the vinegar and olive oil. Add the sugar, oregano, garlic powder, salt, and black pepper, and whisk until blended.

To prepare the salad, gently toss the arugula, carrots, raspberries, and walnuts together in a large bowl. Top with the cheese. Serve the dressing with the salad. Store leftover dressing in the refrigerator for up to 3 days.

Makes 1 1/2 cups of dressing and 4 servings of salad.

June's Walnut and Grape Chicken Salad

It seemed as though Mom always had this chicken salad in the refrigerator, and she would serve it to guests or family. It never lasted long, and she was always making more.

3 boneless, skinless chicken breasts
2 boneless, skinless chicken thighs
(Alternately, use 4 to 5 cups
   leftover chicken, chopped)
1 cup mayonnaise
1/2 cup chopped sweet onions (like Walla
   Walla, Vidalia, or Texas Sweet)

1/2 teaspoon poppy seeds
1 celery rib, finely chopped
1/4 cup chopped walnuts
Salt and black pepper to taste
1 cup green seedless grapes, quartered

Preheat the oven to 375 degrees.

    Place the chicken pieces on a broiler pan. Place the pan in the oven, and bake for 20 minutes or until well done. The chicken is done when its juices run clear when pierced with a fork. Remove the chicken from the oven, and let cool to room temperature. Once cooled, chop the chicken into small pieces, and place in a large bowl.

    Add the mayonnaise, onions, poppy seeds, celery, and walnuts. Add salt and black pepper to taste. Stir in the grapes. Refrigerate for at least 45 minutes before serving.

Makes 8 servings.

Heart-Healthy Apple Tuna Salad

Mom would often serve her tuna salad with fresh, sliced garden tomatoes, salt-and-pepper matzo crackers, and sharp white Cheddar cheese on the side.

2 hard-cooked eggs
2 (5-ounce) cans albacore tuna
   in spring water, drained
1 cup mayonnaise (or less if desired)

½ cup finely chopped sweet onions (like
   Walla Walla, Vidalia, or Texas Sweet)
1 medium red apple, peeled,
   cored, and finely chopped
Salt and black pepper to taste

Peel the eggs, slice them in half, and remove the yolks. Discard the yolks or save for another use. Finely chop the egg whites. Place the egg whites and tuna in a medium bowl. Stir in the mayonnaise, onions, and apple. Add the salt and black pepper to taste. Refrigerate for at least 45 minutes before serving.

Makes 4 servings.

Rosanne Cash's New York Summer Potato Salad

My sister Rosanne Cash has lived in New York City since 1991. The city is a huge part of her life—its culture, art, music, and, of course, the food. New York has some of the finest restaurants in the world and is host to the specific tastes of a thousand cultures of vast ethnic diversity. Rosanne has cooked her whole life and shares this recipe as a taste of the city itself. It reminds me of my childhood years visiting New York City. To make a delicious Cash-Carter crossover dish, use Maybelle Carter's Home-Canned Half-Sour Pickles (recipe on page 59). Thanks to Roseanne's unique twists, this is my very favorite potato salad.

3 pounds red potatoes, unpeeled

4 hard-cooked eggs

1 cup chopped celery

3 to 4 large kosher dill pickles, coarsely chopped (about 1 1/2 cups)

1 medium red onion, finely chopped

Pinch of celery salt

3/4 cup mayonnaise

2 tablespoons Dijon mustard

Salt and black pepper to taste

Place the potatoes in a large pot and cover with water. Bring to a boil over medium-high heat, and cook until tender, about 30 minutes. Drain the potatoes, remove from the pot, and allow them to cool in a large bowl. Cut the potatoes into cubes, and return to the bowl.

Peel the eggs, cut them in half, and remove the yolks. Chop the egg whites and yolks separately. Add the chopped whites and yolks to the potatoes. Add the celery, pickles, onions, and celery salt. Add the mayonnaise and mustard, and stir well. Add the salt and black pepper to taste. Cover and refrigerate. I like to let this salad stand for 1 hour at room temperature before serving.

Makes 8 to 10 servings.

Zesty and Spicy Chipotle Guacamole

I like to serve this guacamole in a molcajete, a Mexican bowl made of black volcanic stone that resembles a mortar and pestle.

1 medium jalapeño pepper

4 ripe avocados

1 medium tomato, diced

3 tablespoons finely chopped sweet onion
   (like Walla Walla, Vidalia, or Texas Sweet)

1 tablespoon finely chopped garlic

Juice of 1/2 lime

Juice of 1/2 lemon

Salt and black pepper to taste

2 tablespoons chopped cilantro

Heat a small skillet over medium heat, and place the whole jalapeño in the pan. Roast the jalapeño, turning occasionally. When it is slightly charred and beginning to smoke, remove the pan from the heat, and allow the jalapeño to cool.

Cut the avocados in half and remove the seeds. Using a small, sharp knife, cut the avocados while in their skins, spoon out the pulp, and place in a serving bowl. Add the tomatoes, onion, and garlic, and mix well with a fork to mash the avocado.

Remove the seeds from the jalapeño, dice, and add it to the avocado mixture. Add the lime and lemon juices. Add the salt and black pepper to taste. Top with the cilantro before serving. Serve with corn chips.

Makes about 2 cups.

Southern-Style Sausage and Cheese Balls

1 pound Southern-style breakfast sausage

1 (16-ounce) package shredded
   mild Cheddar cheese

2 cups baking mix (like Bisquick)

Preheat the oven to 350 degrees.

    Combine the sausage, cheese, and baking mix in a large bowl, and blend well. Roll out small balls in your hand, a little bit smaller than the size of a Ping-Pong ball. Place the balls on a large cookie sheet or broiler pan. Place the sheet in the oven, and bake for 25 minutes, or until sausage is well done and the balls are browned. Remove and serve while still hot.

Makes 30 to 40.

JOHN CARTER'S TIP: You can prebake the balls for 10 minutes, and then let them cool and freeze them in a plastic bag. When ready to serve, reheat the frozen balls on a cookie sheet in a 400-degree oven for about 15 minutes, or until hot and nicely browned.

Joseph Cash's Baked Cheddar and Chive Nachos with Refried Beans

My oldest son, Joseph Cash, is now twenty-two years old. He is on his own, in college, and doesn't have a lot of time for cooking. Between his music, acting, and classes, he barely has time for a quick bite to eat. This is an easy and delicious meal for a college kid on the move or even for the whole family. It also makes for great party fare.

1 (13-ounce) bag corn chips

1 (16-ounce) can refried beans

1/2 cup chopped chives or sweet onions (like Walla Walla, Vidalia, or Texas Sweet)

1 (16-ounce) package shredded sharp Cheddar cheese

1/2 cup diced tomatoes

1/2 cup seeded and diced jalapeño peppers

1 sprig cilantro, chopped

Salt and black pepper to taste

1/4 cup sour cream, optional

Preheat the oven to 350 degrees.

Spread the corn chips evenly on a jelly-roll pan. Scatter the refried beans and chives on top of the chips. Cover with the shredded cheese. Place the pan in the oven, and bake for 15 minutes, or until cheese is melted and beginning to brown. Remove from the oven.

Combine the tomatoes, jalapeños, cilantro, and salt and black pepper to taste in a small bowl. Scatter the tomato mixture over the nachos. Spoon dollops of the sour cream evenly over the nachos, if using. Serve while still hot.

Makes 8 to 10 servings.

Johnny's Roasted Peanuts

One of my dad's favorite snacks was peanuts; he loved peanuts and peanut butter. If he could find green peanuts, he would roast them himself. Throughout his life, I remember Dad pinching the skin on his arm and saying to me, "See that? Peanuts!" He loved peanuts.

Green peanuts are sometimes hard to come by, but if you can find them, they're an easy-to-prepare, delicious, and healthy treat. Dad made them several times a year, every year of our life together, so their wondrous aroma was quite typical around our home.

1 to 2 pounds raw green peanuts   **Salt and black pepper**

Preheat the oven to 350 degrees.

Spread the raw peanuts on a jelly-roll pan, and sprinkle them with salt and pepper. Place the pan in the oven, and bake for 10 minutes. Open the oven and shake the pan, rolling the peanuts around so that they roast evenly. Continue roasting for another 5 to 10 minutes, until the peanut shells are a rich brown. Remove from the oven, and let cool before serving. Shell the peanuts if desired.

Makes 2 3/4 to 3 cups of in-the-shell peanuts.

Ana Cristina Cash's Prosciutto-Wrapped Dates with Goat Cheese

I met my wife, Ana Cristina, in October of 2013. At first, there was no romance whatsoever, just an easy camaraderie and kinship. It was almost a year later, in late 2014, that Ana Cristina and I had our first date, and since then, we have been steadfast and in love.

Ana is of Cuban descent, her parents having immigrated to Miami from Cuba in the 1960s. She speaks perfect Spanish, is a master vocalist, songwriter, and performer, and is humble, kind, and generous. We married on October 29, 2016, in Charleston, South Carolina, in an unforgettable and magical ceremony.

On our third date, Ana cooked a delicious meal for me: a slow-roasted chicken with sage—to die for (a recipe for another time). Among the hors d'oeuvres before the meal were these simple Prosciutto-Wrapped Dates with Goat Cheese.

We serve them regularly at our home to this day, and it always takes me back to the time our love was just beginning.

Cooking spray or vegetable oil	**1 (8-ounce) package soft goat cheese**
16 ounces pitted dates	**1 (8-ounce) package thinly sliced prosciutto**

Preheat the oven to 350 degrees. Coat a large cookie sheet with cooking spray or vegetable oil.

Break open the dates, and fill with a small dab of goat cheese. Close the dates back up, and wrap them with small strips of prosciutto, skewering with toothpicks as you go. Place the dates on the sheet. Place the cookie sheet in the oven, and bake for 15 minutes, or until the prosciutto is beginning to brown. Serve while still warm.

Makes 6 to 8 servings.

Jamaican Cheese Soufflé

At my parents' home in Jamaica, called Cinnamon Hill, we had a chef who had studied at Le Cordon Bleu in London. She was Jamaican, and "Ms. Edith" was one of the finest cooks I have ever known. She, of course, made the classic Jamaican dishes but also prepared wondrous creations of her own inspiration. This soufflé is as close to her recipe as I have been able to copy. I recall the slight bite of the Scotch bonnet, certainly not too hot, but just right. And I recall the taste of the allspice, but only if your serving contained a scraping from the sides of the pan. Jamaican allspice (called pimenta by Jamaicans) is akin to cloves, not the mild pepper pimento that we typically see stuffed in olives.

There was a large oak table in the Cinnamon Hill dining room, and I cannot eat this soufflé without being transported back to that table and those years of my childhood—my parents, visitors, guests, and other family fellowshipping in that long mahogany-floored room in which we dined. But what comes to mind most of all is the fine food laid upon it.

1 tablespoon plus ¼ cup
   unsalted butter, divided
½ tablespoon finely grated Parmesan cheese
Pinch of Jamaican allspice
¼ cup all-purpose flour
2 drops of Jamaican Scotch bonnet pepper
   sauce or habanero pepper sauce, optional
¼ teaspoon salt

1 ¼ cups whole milk
¼ cup shredded Gruyère cheese
¾ cup sharp white Cheddar cheese
   (New Zealand Cheddar is preferred)
6 large eggs, room temperature
   and separated
¼ teaspoon cream of tartar

Preheat the oven to 375 degrees. Melt 1 tablespoon of the butter, and rub around a 2-quart soufflé pan or two 1-quart pans. Dust the Parmesan cheese and the allspice evenly around the pan. It should stick to the butter.

In a separate large pan, melt ¼ cup of the butter over medium heat, and just when it starts bubbling, add the flour. Make sure not to brown the flour, just heat and stir to the point where it is creamy. Stir in the pepper sauce, salt, and milk, and bring back to a boil, stirring constantly. Just as soon as it boils, remove it from the heat.

Add the Gruyère and Cheddar cheeses, and stir well until melted. Beat the egg yolks until blended, and add to the cheese mixture, stirring until smooth.

In a separate large bowl, beat the egg whites using an electric mixer on low until foamy. Add cream of tartar, then continue beating at high speed, until stiff peaks form. This may take a little while, but you'll know you have the correct consistency when you can dip a spoon into the whites and stiff peaks form when you raise it up.

Add a quarter of the cheese mixture to the egg whites, and gently fold in until blended. Repeat three more times. (Stir too much and you'll have a flat soufflé.)

Scrape the mixture into the baking pan or pans. Fill to within three-fourths from the top at least, but never fill all the way. Any higher and it could spill over when it cooks.

If you want a dramatic crown on your soufflé, make a ring of foil to attach around the rim. How tall the foil needs to be depends on how much higher you fill your pan. (Around our house, we just like to eat the dish and don't care as much about how it looks. But if you want to make a "crowning glory" at the top, it may be a trial-and-error affair until you get it to your satisfaction.)

Bake the soufflé about 30 minutes, until it is browned and looks crispy with a few cracks here and there. (Turn on your oven light and watch closely.) Carefully remove from the oven to avoid shaking it too much and causing it to fall. Serve immediately.

Makes 4 servings.

Jack's Spicy Moose Jerky

My son Jack has an exceedingly adventuresome palate. When he was quite young, we would take him to sushi restaurants. Each and every visit he would order "sea grapes." The server would inevitably look at Jack with confusion.

"We don't have grapes here, sorry" was the typical response. I would go on to explain he meant the brine-preserved Japanese-style salmon eggs called ikura. The server would smile, inspired that such a young man would have such an expanded palate. When his order arrived, Jack would dig right in. Though his etiquette was certainly not prime, it was worth it all to see the surprised faces of the restaurant patrons as the unflinching child lifted one egg at a time to his mouth, popping each with his teeth. They were, and still are, his favorite item on a sushi menu.

Jack's sister AnnaBelle has similarly audacious tastes. When she was two years old, she was sitting in a high chair at a sushi bar. I ordered a large plate of tuna sashimi. After it was served, I turned away for a minute to chat with my friend. When I turned back, AnnaBelle had grabbed a handful of tuna and was just finishing a monstrous bite. I quickly pulled it away. Perhaps she thought it was Jell-O; I don't know. But she loves sushi to this day, and one of her favorite orders is the freshest tuna sashimi.

Jack helps me in the kitchen, and a few years back, after a hunting trip to Newfoundland, we found ourselves with an abundance of moose meat in our large deep freezer. We had often made both venison and beef jerky, but Jack decided to make a special marinade for this rare moose meat. We made around ten pounds of this jerky, seasoning some of it hotter than other batches. I will never forget its particular taste. Here is Jack's recipe that he wrote out by hand himself.

1 cup Worcestershire sauce

½ cup spicy barbecue sauce (Center Point barbecue sauce from Hendersonville, Tennessee, if available. If not, Stubb's or Sweet Baby Ray's. The jerky is best if the sauce is not too sweet.)

⅓ cup soy sauce

¼ cup raw or regular honey

½ cup Coca-Cola, not diet

2 tablespoons garlic powder

2 tablespoons cayenne pepper

1 teaspoon ground cinnamon

2 tablespoons ground cumin

2 tablespoons chili powder

2 pounds thinly sliced lean moose meat (venison, elk, or lean beef if no moose is available)

Combine the Worcestershire, barbecue sauce, soy sauce, honey, cola, garlic powder, cayenne pepper, cinnamon, cumin, and chili powder in a large bowl, and stir well. Place the meat in a zip-top plastic bag. Pour in the marinade. Close the bag and massage the mixture into the meat. Refrigerate overnight.

Place the meat strips on dehydrator trays and follow your dehydrator's directions, or use your favorite oven method for making jerky. As an example, preheat the oven to 250 degrees. Place a baking rack in a jelly-roll pan. Drain the meat from the marinade and pat dry with paper towels. Arrange the meat on the rack in a single layer. Bake for about 4 hours, until dry to the touch. Remove from the oven and let dry in a cool, dry place for another 24 hours.

Makes about one pound.

Maybelle Carter's Home-Canned Half-Sour Pickles

Most of the world eats a great deal of fermented food, and some of those recipes have made their way into our diets here in the United States. The helpful enzymes and bacteria in fermented foods help with digestion and, according to some experts, many other ailments as well. Yogurt is an example of a popular fermented food here in the United States. In Korea, kimchi is a favorite; in Germany it's sauerkraut. Then there's tempeh in Indonesia and natto in Japan. I would venture to say that the most regularly consumed fermented food here in America is pickles.

Two of the more common varieties are kosher dill and half-sour pickles. Kosher pickles are fermented in a brine for a long period, while half-sour pickles are fermented for a shorter amount of time, leaving the cucumber crisp and tasty.

"Mother" Maybelle Carter first visited New York City in the 1930s while recording music with the Carter Family. She told my mother it was then and there that she first tasted a half-sour pickle. "She went to Ben's Kosher Deli," Mom said. "She had a pastrami sandwich with mustard on rye bread and had a pickle with the sandwich."

Mom went on to tell me that Maybelle had long made pickles in the valley where they lived, but she had used a thick brine with vinegar and sugar. These "city pickles" were different.

One thing that was paramount in the area where my grandmother grew up in Maces Spring, Virginia, were fresh ingredients. Grandma had a spring rising from the base of the mountain right there in her backyard. She grew Kirby cucumbers and knew that when they were picked at just the right time, they made the perfect half-sour pickle. She also had wild muscadine vines (a native grape in the South) in the woods just behind the house, and she used the leaves of these vines to add tannins to her pickles.

There was also a cellar in Maybelle's house, and the pickles she made would last for months stored in that cellar.

This is my grandmother's version of those "city pickles" she first had in New York City. You'll need a half-gallon glass Mason or Ball jar and a glass fermentation weight for this recipe.

Small to medium whole Kirby or other heirloom cucumbers, just enough to fill the jar (uniform size if possible)

4 tablespoons plus 3/4 teaspoon kosher salt

2 quarts bottled spring water or another type of water with absolutely no chlorine

2 large bunches fresh dill
Garlic
2 tablespoons coriander seeds
1 tablespoon mustard seeds

½ tablespoon black peppercorns
3 to 6 oak, grape, or muscadine leaves or
   2 tablespoons strawberry leaves

Cut just the tops of the cucumbers off.

In a large bowl mix together the salt with the water, and stir until dissolved.

Add a third of the dill, garlic, coriander seeds, mustard seeds, and peppercorns to the jar, plus half of the leaves. Then pack in the cucumbers to the halfway mark on the jar. (Packing the cucumbers can be an art; be careful not to bruise the crunchy vegetables in the process.)

Add another third of the dill, garlic, coriander seeds, mustard seeds, and peppercorns, and all but one of the leaves. Fill the jar with the remaining cucumbers, to within ½ inch of the top of the jar. Add the remaining dill, garlic, coriander seeds, mustard seeds, and peppercorns, plus one final leaf. Pour the brine solution over the pickles, completely covering them.

Push the fermentation weight on top of the cucumbers, fully submerging them in the brine. (Using the glass weight ensures that none of the cucumbers are exposed to the air where they are vulnerable to bacteria.) Cover the jar with a breathable cloth, like cheesecloth, and secure with a rubber band. Let sit at room temperature for 4 to 5 days; the longer the fermentation, the less crispy the pickle. Once done fermenting, cover the jar with a metal lid, and refrigerate. These pickles can last for months in the fridge.

Makes 1/2 gallon.

JOHN CARTER'S TIP: Fermentation weights are heavy and thick pieces of glass, typically round, to fit in the top of a Mason jar.

John Carter's American Kimchi

Kimchi, another fermented food, has long been one of my favorites. I first ate it in New York City, in Koreatown, not too far from the Empire State Building. Traditionally made with Korean hot chili peppers, I tried this North American chili pepper variation and loved it. You'll need a half-gallon glass Mason or Ball jar and a glass fermentation weight for this recipe.

When using fresh chili peppers, the longer you ferment this kimchi, the hotter and stronger the taste. Taste it at four days to see if you like it. Let it ferment longer if desired, tasting every few days until the mixture reaches the flavor you prefer.

4 large jalapeño peppers

5 serrano peppers

1 habanero pepper

5 garlic cloves

2 tablespoons raw or regular honey

1/4 cup warm water

7 tablespoons kosher salt

2 quarts bottled spring water or another
 type of water with absolutely no chlorine

1 large head Napa cabbage, chopped

Wearing rubber gloves, wash the peppers, and cut off the stems. Place the peppers in the bowl of a food processor. Add the garlic. In a small bowl combine the honey and warm water, and stir until blended. Add the honey mixture to the food processor.

Combine the salt and spring water in a large pitcher, and stir until dissolved. Pour in enough of the salt water to just cover the pepper mixture in the food processor. Process until finely pureed.

Place the cabbage in a half-gallon glass jar. Pour the pepper mixture over the cabbage. Add the remaining salt water, and press the mixture down with a glass fermentation weight. Let stand at room temperature at least 4 days and up to 2 weeks, depending on how strong you want the kimchi to taste.

Store covered in the refrigerator. The flavors will continue to evolve. Kimchi can last up to a year if kept between 33 and 35 degrees.

Makes approximately 1/2 gallon.

Jamaican Scotch Bonnet Hot Pepper Sauce

1 pound whole Scotch bonnet or
   habanero peppers, stems removed
2 1/2 tablespoons salt
1/2 cup chopped yellow onions

3 garlic cloves
1 1/2 cups cider vinegar
2 tablespoons pure cane sugar or white
   sugar

Place the peppers and salt in the bowl of a food processor, and process until chopped into small pieces. Transfer the mixture into a 1-quart Mason jar, and let stand, loosely covered, for 6 hours or overnight.

Place the onions and garlic in the bowl of a food processor, and pulse until chopped. Add the mixture to the peppers. Pour in the vinegar and sugar, and stir well. Let stand for 3 to 5 days at room temperature, loosely covered.

Pour the pepper mixture into the bowl of a food processor, and process until pureed. Return the mixture to the jar, and cover tightly. Store in the refrigerator up to 3 months. Shake before each use, and use sparingly. This sauce is very, very hot!

Makes about 2 1/2 cups.

JOHN CARTER'S TIP: Careful! These peppers are dangerous to touch. The oils can irritate or burn your skin, face, or eyes, so it's a good idea to wear rubber gloves when handling these peppers.

Cash and Carter Ring of Fire Barbecue Sauce

The taste of love is sweet
When hearts like ours meet . . .
And it burns, burns, burns,
The ring of fire, the ring of fire.
—June Carter Cash and Merle Kilgore

2 cups tomato ketchup
1 cup cider vinegar
1 cup water
1 cup firmly packed brown sugar
1/2 cup raw or regular honey
3 tablespoons Worcestershire sauce
1/2 tablespoon mustard powder

1/2 teaspoon garlic powder
1 teaspoon onion powder
1/2 teaspoon paprika
1/4 teaspoon black pepper
Dash of habanero pepper sauce
1/2 teaspoon cayenne pepper, optional

Combine the ketchup, vinegar, water, brown sugar, honey, Worcestershire, mustard powder, garlic powder, onion powder, paprika, black pepper, pepper sauce, and cayenne pepper, if using, in a large saucepan. Bring to a boil over medium-high heat. Reduce the heat to low, and simmer the mixture for 20 minutes, stirring often. Let cool before serving with your favorite barbecue recipe. Store in a sealed container in the refrigerator for up to 3 weeks.

Makes about 3 1/2 cups.

Sesame Soy Pineapple Marinade

Use this marinade for chicken, beef, or wild game. Place the meat and the marinade in a large zip-top plastic bag, and refrigerate for 2 hours for chicken or 2 hours to overnight for beef or wild game.

1 cup soy sauce
1/2 cup pineapple juice
1/2 teaspoon ground ginger

1/2 teaspoon garlic powder
1/8 teaspoon allspice
1/8 teaspoon sesame oil

Combine the soy sauce, pineapple juice, ground ginger, garlic powder, allspice, and sesame oil in a medium bowl. Whisk together well.

Makes 1 1/2 cups.

Cash's Spicy Tartar Sauce

½ cup mayonnaise

1 tablespoon finely diced sweet onion (like Walla Walla, Vidalia, or Texas Sweet)

Juice of ½ lemon

1 teaspoon yellow mustard

½ teaspoon minced fresh tarragon or ¼ teaspoon dried

1 teaspoon minced capers

Dash of Louisiana-style hot pepper sauce or to taste

Combine the mayonnaise, onions, lemon juice, mustard, tarragon, capers, and hot sauce in a small bowl. Stir well. Refrigerate for at least 1 hour, and stir well before serving.

Makes about ½ cup.

CHAPTER 3

Side Dishes and Memorable Main Courses

Mom was never without respect for etiquette; there was never a "casual sit down." She would set the same fine table for every single meal, and eating dinner on a plate in front of the television would have been completely unacceptable. She even took me to an etiquette class in New York City once when we were there on an extended stay during the years we had an apartment there. I was ten years old and wanted to go to the movies and to Central Park, wander around the zoo and FAO Schwartz, or perhaps visit the Natural History Museum. But my dear mother had other ideas!

New York City is a place where most anything can be found, if you look for it, and a class on teaching little children how to set a table was no exception. She found a three-day class for kids my age at a culinary institute on the Upper West Side, and she took me there each day of the class, sat in the back, and listened intently. She knew very well what I was being taught and had used the proper setting patterns since she was a little girl. Mom told me that her mother, Maybelle, had taught her to set a table from a diagram out of a book by Emily Post. It happened to be that we were using that exact same book in the class that day. At the beginning of the class they gave us that diagram to take home with us. Mom had me practice it every day for a week.

Wild Turkey Roulade

Like the rest of the kids in the etiquette class I attended in New York City as a boy, I fidgeted in my seat, tapping a steel spoon and butter knife on a porcelain plate while the instructor recited a well-memorized lecture. Occasionally my mother, sitting in the back of the room, would clear her throat, perhaps making sure I was listening and reminding me in her own way to sit still. But I didn't fidget for long, as after the first half hour, the instructor gave us the opportunity to learn to cook a main course.

It was a turkey roulade, a dish I had never had. I loved it. I have since made this delicious dish many times through the years. When available, I use wild turkey as the meat, though fresh domestic turkey breast works fine too.

1 (1-pound) wild or domestic turkey breast
Sea salt and black pepper
8 ounces thinly sliced prosciutto
   (about 8 slices)
8 basil leaves
8 sage leaves

8 ounces thinly sliced provolone
   cheese (about 8 slices)
4 tablespoons non-pareil capers
4 ounces Gruyère cheese, shredded
4 tablespoons butter

Preheat the oven to 375 degrees.

Slice the turkey breast into two long pieces, and pound each piece until about 1/4 inch thick. Sprinkle the turkey with salt and black pepper. Place the prosciutto slices, in one layer, over each turkey slice. Scatter the basil and sage on top of the prosciutto. Place the cheese slices on top of the leaves.

Roll each turkey stack like a jelly roll into a roulade. Place the roulades in a shallow baking pan. Sprinkle the capers and Gruyère cheese on top of the roulades, and place pats of butter on top.

Cover the pan with foil. Place the pan in the oven, and bake for 25 minutes. Remove the foil, and increase the oven temperature to 400 degrees. Bake for 10 minutes, or until the cheese is golden brown. Slice and serve immediately.

Makes 4 to 6 servings.

Cash Family Cornbread

Just like biscuits and gravy, cornbread was everyday fare around the Cash home. Dad loved Southern cornbread, and one of his very favorite meals was cornbread crumbled up in a tall glass of buttermilk—to be eaten with a spoon. It may be an acquired taste, but most everyone in my family enjoys cornbread and buttermilk as a delicious treat.

If you can't find self-rising cornmeal mix (and it's often hard to find outside of the South), you can use regular cornmeal and add flour, baking powder, and salt as outlined in this recipe.

This cornbread goes great with Johnny's Pinto Beans and Ham Hocks or with your own version of Ezra Carter's "Sunbitchin' Stew." (Recipes on pages 82 and 94.)

2 cups self-rising cornmeal mix (or
    1 1/2 cups white cornmeal, 1/2 cup all-
    purpose flour, 2 teaspoons baking
    powder, and 1 teaspoon salt)
3/4 cup shortening, divided
1 1/2 cups whole buttermilk
1 large egg

1 tablespoon vegetable oil
3 tablespoons finely diced yellow onions
2 tablespoons finely diced
    jalapeño pepper, optional
1/4 cup shredded sharp white Cheddar
    cheese

Preheat the oven to 450 degrees.

Place the cornmeal mix (or cornmeal, flour, baking powder, and salt) in a large bowl. Stir with a whisk. Add 1/2 cup of the shortening, and using a fork, cut the shortening into the mix until small clumps form. Stir in the buttermilk, egg, and vegetable oil, and mix well. Fold in the onions, jalapeños, if using, and cheese.

Place the remaining 1/4 cup of the shortening in a medium well-seasoned cast-iron skillet or an 8 x 11-inch baking pan. Place the skillet in the oven for 5 minutes, or until the shortening bubbles and cooks the cornmeal batter when a drop is spooned into the skillet. Carefully remove the skillet from the oven, and slowly pour the batter into the hot skillet. Return the skillet to the oven, and cook the cornbread about 30 minutes, until the top is golden brown and a toothpick inserted into the middle comes out clean.

Makes 6 to 8 servings.

JOHN CARTER'S TIP: This cornbread is traditionally made in a cast-iron skillet. If you don't have one, you can still make the cornbread. Just use a heavy nonstick or greased baking pan instead.

John's Soya Grit Bread

3 tablespoons yeast

6 cups warm water (105–110 degrees)

3/4 cup honey

3 tablespoons soybean oil

4 large eggs

7 cups stone ground whole wheat flour

1 1/2 cups soya grits, cooked according to package directions and cooled

1 cup seven grain cereal

1 1/2 cups granola

1/3 cup mixed nuts, crushed

Dash salt

Dissolve the yeast in warm water until the yeast blooms (looks foamy). Stir in the honey, oil, and eggs until blended. Mix the flour, grits, cereal, granola, nuts, and salt in a separate large

continued on next page

JOHNNY CASH

John's Soya Grit Bread

7 Cups Stone Ground Whole Wheat flour

1½ cups Soya Grits

1 cup Soy Flakes

1 cup Seven Grain Cereal

1½ Cup Granola

⅓ cup Mixed Nuts

¾ cup Honey

3 tblsp Soybean Oil

4 Eggs

Vege-salt (to taste)

3 tblsp dry yeast

6 cups water

bowl until combined. Begin to add the flour mixture, a cup at a time, into the yeast mixture, stirring and mixing well. You can use your hands, a wooden spoon, or a stand mixer with a dough hook attached. Once all the dry ingredients are incorporated, knead the dough by hand on a lightly floured surface for about 10 minutes or until it springs to the touch, or continue to mix with the dough hook (on medium speed) for 5 to 6 minutes until the dough springs to the touch.

Cover the dough with cloth, and let it rise till doubled. Punch down and form into two loaves. Place the loaves into well-buttered loaf pans and let rise again for 20 to 30 minutes.

Bake at 350 degrees until loaves rise and are nicely browned on top. Check at 30 minutes, and continue checking every 10 minutes or so. This is a dense bread that may take up to an hour to bake.

Makes 2 loaves.

Johnny's Pinto Beans and Ham Hocks

My father grew up with certain foods that were everyday staples in Dyess, Arkansas, and this was undoubtedly one of them. Beans were perhaps one of the easier foods to come by in hard times, and during the Great Depression of the 1930s and through wartime in the 1940s, the Cash Family got by as they could. Sometimes ham wasn't available, and it was only a pot of beans, typically accompanied by some cornbread (always made with lard back then).

I grew up eating this dish as often as my father did. It was one of his favorite foods his whole life. Dad would always eat it with raw white onions.

1 (16-ounce) bag dried pinto beans
1/2 cup chopped green onions
1 large whole ham hock

1/4 teaspoon cayenne pepper
Salt and black pepper

Rinse the beans, place them in large pot, and cover completely with water. Soak in the refrigerator overnight.

The next day, pour off the water from the bean pan, and add enough water back in the pot to cover the beans by 2 to 2 1/2 inches. Bring the beans to a boil over high heat. Add the onions, ham hock, cayenne pepper, and salt and pepper. Return the beans to a boil, reduce the heat to low, cover the pot, and simmer 2 1/2 to 3 hours, until the beans are tender. Serve hot with coarsely chopped white onions (if desired), Cash Family Cornbread, and perhaps a dash of Jamaican Scotch Bonnet Hot Sauce. (Recipes on pages 76 and 65.)

Makes 6 to 8 servings.

June Carter Cash's "Stuff"

One of the staple dishes of my mother's creation was her unique and memorable "Stuff." I am not sure of its origin, but we ate it even when I was very young. Hot pepper flavor was typical around our house, and to me this dish does not recall my mother's specific handiwork without the pepper jack cheese.

2 to 3 tablespoons vegetable oil
2 large potatoes, peeled and thinly sliced
3 large carrots, peeled and thinly sliced
Salt and black pepper
1 red bell pepper, thinly sliced
½ large sweet onion (like Walla Walla, Vidalia, or Texas Sweet), thinly sliced

2 garlic cloves, thinly sliced
½ cup mushrooms, sliced
1 large zucchini, thinly sliced
2 yellow squash, thinly sliced
1 tablespoon unsalted butter
4 ounces hot pepper jack cheese, shredded

Place the vegetable oil in a large nonstick skillet over medium heat. Add the potatoes and carrots, and sprinkle with salt and black pepper. Cook, stirring often, for 15 minutes. Add the bell pepper, and cook, stirring often, for another 3 minutes. Add the onion and garlic, and cook, stirring often, for 2 minutes. Add the mushrooms, and cook, stirring often, for another 2 or 3 minutes. Then add the zucchini and squash. Add the butter, more salt and black pepper to taste, and simmer for an additional 5 to 8 minutes, until all the vegetables are soft and tender and nicely browned. Reduce the heat to low, and add the cheese. Cover, turn off the heat, and let stand for 10 minutes before serving.

Makes 6 to 8 servings.

Teriyaki and Pancetta Brussels Sprouts

2 tablespoons soy sauce

1 teaspoon raw or regular honey

1/2 teaspoon chopped fresh ginger
    or 1/4 teaspoon ground ginger

2 tablespoons hot water

2 ounces pancetta, coarsely chopped

Dash of olive oil

2 garlic cloves, finely chopped

4 1/2 cups Brussels sprouts, quartered

1 tablespoon water

Fresh-squeezed lemon juice to taste

Salt and black pepper to taste

Crushed red pepper flakes to taste

Combine the soy sauce, honey, ginger, and hot water in a small bowl. Stir well with a fork until the honey dissolves.

Heat a medium skillet over medium-high heat. Add the pancetta and a dash of olive oil to the skillet. Stir-fry until the pancetta begins to brown. Add the garlic, and continue to cook for another minute, before adding the Brussels sprouts. Stir in the water, cover, and reduce the heat to low. Cook for 5 minutes, stirring occasionally. Remove the cover, and add the soy sauce mixture. Continue to cook over low heat, uncovered, until the sauce evaporates and the sprouts are brown and tender. Add the lemon juice, and sprinkle with salt, black pepper, and red pepper flakes. Serve hot.

Makes 4 servings.

Sweet Potato Casserole with Crusty Graham Crackers and Marshmallows

Sweet Potatoes

4 large sweet potatoes, peeled
    and cut into chunks
1 tablespoon salted butter
2 tablespoons raw cane sugar or white sugar
1/4 cup half-and-half

1/2 teaspoon ground cinnamon
1/4 teaspoon ground nutmeg
Pinch of ground cloves
Dash of salt

Topping

1/4 cup firmly packed brown sugar
1/2 cup unsalted butter, melted
1/4 cup graham cracker crumbs
2 tablespoons all-purpose flour
1/4 teaspoon ground cinnamon

Pinch of ground nutmeg
Pinch of salt
4 ounces chopped pecans
2 1/2 cups mini marshmallows, divided

Preheat the oven to 375 degrees. Butter a 9 x 13-inch casserole dish.

To prepare the sweet potatoes, place them in the dish, adding a shallow layer of water to the bottom. Place the dish in the oven, and bake about 30 minutes, until the sweet potatoes begin to soften. Remove from the oven, drain the water from the dish, and spoon out the sweet potato pieces into a large bowl.

Add the butter, sugar, half-and-half, cinnamon, nutmeg, cloves, and salt. Blend with an electric hand mixer until smooth. Return the mixture to the dish, and place back in the oven. Bake for 4 to 5 minutes, until the mixture is steaming and heated through.

To prepare the topping, combine the brown sugar, butter, graham cracker crumbs, flour, cinnamon, nutmeg, salt, pecans, and half of the marshmallows in a medium saucepan. Stir well and cook over medium heat until the mixture begins to bubble and the marshmallows and sugar melt together.

Spread a layer of the marshmallow mixture over the top of the sweet potatoes. Return the sweet potatoes to the oven, and bake for 12 to 14 minutes. Remove the dish from the oven, and add the remaining marshmallows. Return to the oven, and bake until the marshmallows are browned and the crust is browned. Serve hot.

Makes 4 to 6 servings.

Damon's Nomad Special Asparagus with Almonds and Garlic

This special asparagus dish was a favorite of my cousin Damon's and a regular side at his house. Damon was my aunt Louise's son on my father's side, and he and my dad were quite close. Damon walks like my father, talks like my father, and in many ways, acts like Dad.

Damon was once a water polo champion and a policeman in Southern California. Among other accomplishments, he was the 1965 Western States Family Police Force Iron Man champion, victor and winner of the Brass Knuckles Top Man Trophy at the 1966 Deschutes High Desert Arm Wrestling Face-Off, and holder of twelve blue, gold, and pink ribbons for baking and pickling between 1961 and 1967 at regional and state fairs in Nevada, Utah, and California. This recipe is for you, Damon.

2 tablespoons olive oil
2 tablespoons sliced almonds
2 garlic cloves, peeled and crushed

1 bunch green asparagus,
   tough ends removed
Salt and black pepper to taste

In a medium skillet heat the olive oil over medium heat. Add the almonds, and cook, stirring constantly, until they begin to brown, 4 or 5 minutes. Remove the almonds from the pan. Add the garlic to the pan, and cook, stirring constantly, until it begins to brown, 2 to 3 minutes. Add the asparagus. Cover the pan, and reduce the heat to low. Cook for 3 to 5 minutes, flip the asparagus, cover again, and cook for another 3 to 5 minutes on the other side. Add the salt and black pepper to taste and the almonds, stirring together once or twice. Serve hot.

Makes 4 to 6 servings.

> **DAMON'S TIP:** You decide how long you want to cook the asparagus. I prefer mine tender but with a slight "bite." If you prefer it softer, cook it longer. I think asparagus is best when it's not cooked to sogginess.

Cash Family Beef Pot Roast with Potatoes and Carrots

Salt and black pepper
1 (2 1/2-pound) beef roast
1/2 cup all-purpose flour
3 tablespoons vegetable oil or shortening
3 cups water, divided
2 large baking potatoes, cut
    into 1- to 2-inch chunks
2 celery stalks, cut into 1- to 2-inch pieces

1 1/2 cups sliced carrots (about 3 to 4 carrots)
1/2 large sweet onion, chopped
    into 1- to 2-inch pieces
3 cloves garlic, finely chopped
2 sprigs fresh parsley or 2 to
    3 teaspoons dried parsley
1/2 teaspoon rubbed sage
Pinch of salt and black pepper

Heat the oven to 375 degrees.

Generously salt and pepper the roast on all sides, then dredge in flour. Heat the oil in a large Dutch oven, or other heavy-duty ovenproof baking pan, on the stove over medium heat. Brown the roast in the pan on all sides (3 to 4 minutes on each side or until a rich brown).

Remove the roast from the pan and set aside. Add the remainder of the flour to the pan. Stirring constantly, brown the flour, adding a bit more oil if needed, being careful not to burn the flour. Whisk in 1 1/2 cups water, stirring and cooking on medium-high heat until the gravy begins to thicken.

Return the roast to the pan, then turn off the heat and add all the potatoes, celery, carrots, onions, garlic, parsley, and sage. Add the remainder of the water to the pan to almost cover the vegetables. Sprinkle with a pinch of salt and pepper.

Cover and cook in the oven at 375 degrees for 20 minutes, then turn the heat down to 285 degrees and cook for another 5 hours or until the roast and vegetables are tender.

Serve with Cash Family Cornbread. (Recipe on page 76.)

Makes 4 to 6 servings.

Ezra Carter's "Sunbitchin' Stew"

Each day's cooking in a traditional country home included a combination of wondrous foods. The day may have begun with farm-fresh tomatoes served with free-range eggs, biscuits, country ham, and all the fixins. Lunch probably would have been more meager, as the midday meal was meant to strengthen, not lay out, the family who had been working hard in the fields or with the livestock all morning. Perhaps lunch was a slice of bread with a dab of peanut butter, covered with homemade jam or honey from the farm's hives. Dinner, on the other hand, when affordable, could be a hearty affair, especially on Sundays. That's the day the family would gather 'round the dining table and, after a prayer, dive into generous servings of black-eyed peas, cornbread, fried chicken, squash casserole, green beans with ham hocks, or perhaps baked ham with sweet potatoes, likely finished off with apple, peach, or cherry pie for dessert.

Leftovers, whether meager or abundant, were never wasted. And it was the leftovers that begged my grandfather Ezra to create his unique and ever-changing Sunbitchin' Stew.

Since the very nature of this dish is based on what's left over, the variations are endless. This is just an example of what you can do!

2 1/2 tablespoons olive oil

1/4 cup chopped onion

2 garlic cloves, finely chopped

1/2 cup corn kernels, fresh or leftover, or a heaping tablespoon of leftover corn casserole

2 cups beef or chicken stock

1 cup chopped or shredded leftover chicken or roast turkey or 1 cup cooked and drained ground beef or venison or 3 finely chopped leftover hamburger patties

1/2 cup chopped cooked ham or leftover or fresh chopped smoked sausage pieces, bratwurst, kielbasa, or andouille

1/2 cup lima beans

1/2 cup green beans or a heaping tablespoon of leftover green bean casserole

1/2 cup leftover baked potatoes, chopped, or a heaping tablespoon of leftover mashed potatoes

1/2 cup sweet potato casserole or a heaping tablespoon of leftover candied yams

1 (8-ounce) can tomato sauce

2 large tomatoes, chopped

1 teaspoon paprika

2 teaspoons mild chili powder

1/4 teaspoon rubbed sage or 1 teaspoon fresh chopped sage

1/4 teaspoon dried oregano or 2 teaspoons chopped fresh oregano

¼ teaspoon ground thyme or
   1 teaspoon chopped fresh thyme
Salt and black pepper to taste

¼ teaspoon cayenne pepper, or to taste
½ cup leftover cooked rice or pasta or both
   (if using pasta, chop into small pieces)

Heat the oil over medium heat in a large pot. Add the onions and garlic. Cook, stirring, until the onions become translucent and the garlic takes on a slight brown hint, for 2 or 3 minutes.

Add the corn, and cook, stirring, for another minute. Pour in the stock, increase the heat to medium-high, and bring to a boil.

Add the chicken and ham. Stir in the lima beans, green beans, potatoes, and sweet potatoes. Stir well, and add the tomato sauce and tomatoes. Reduce the heat to low, and add the paprika, chili powder, sage, oregano, thyme, salt and black pepper to taste, and cayenne pepper, if using. Simmer for 20 minutes, stirring every 5 minutes or so. Add the rice or pasta. Simmer for another 5 minutes, and serve immediately.

Makes 8 to 10 servings.

Barbecue Pulled Pork with Orange-Honey Glaze

1 (2- to 3-pound) pork shoulder roast
Salt and black pepper
1/2 cup apple juice

1/2 cup firmly packed brown sugar, divided
4 1/2 cups cola
3/4 cup orange juice, divided

Spread several layers of heavy-duty foil onto a sturdy jelly-roll pan. You want enough foil to come up the sides and all the way around your roast. Place the pork roast on the foil, and generously sprinkle with salt and black pepper on all sides. Turn up the sides of the foil until a cradle is created.

In a separate bowl, mix together the apple juice, 1/4 cup of the brown sugar, the cola, and 1/2 cup of the orange juice. Stir until the sugar begins to dissolve, and pour over the roast.

Wrap the foil tightly around the roast. You can either place the foil-covered roast on a grill and cook over indirect, low heat for 5 to 7 hours, or you can bake it in a 275-degree oven for 6 hours. If baking in the oven, it's a good idea to place the foil-covered roast on a sturdy baking pan to prevent juices from seeping out into the oven.

Remove the roast from the grill or oven, carefully open the foil package, and let the roast cool. Once cooled, remove the pork from the foil, and shred the meat with two forks. Mix the cooking juices from the foil cradle in with the pulled pork, and return the pork to the cradle.

In a small bowl mix together the remaining 1/4 cup of brown sugar and 1/4 cup of orange juice, and pour over the pulled pork. Return the pork, uncovered, to the grill, and grill over high heat for 20 minutes or until browned and crispy. If using the oven, broil, uncovered, until browned and crispy. Serve with Cash and Carter Ring of Fire Barbecue Sauce. (Recipe on page 66.)

Makes 6 servings.

JOHN CARTER'S TIP: The safest way to cook any meat is to use a meat thermometer. For lamb, rare is 125 degrees, medium-rare is 130 to 135 degrees, and medium is 135 to 140 degrees.

Roast Leg of Lamb with Garlic Crust and Fresh Mint Sauce

Lamb

1 (3- to 4 1/2-pound) boneless leg of lamb
Salt and black pepper
1/2 teaspoon ground thyme

1/2 teaspoon rubbed sage
4 garlic cloves, crushed

Mint Sauce

Large handful fresh mint leaves
1/4 cup boiling water
1/2 teaspoon salt

3 tablespoons white wine vinegar
2 tablespoons sugar

To prepare the lamb, preheat the oven to 400 degrees.

Cut several parallel 1/4-inch-deep slits in the top of the leg of lamb, 4 to 5 inches long. Rub the meat with a generous amount of salt and black pepper. Coat the meat evenly with the thyme and sage. Rub the crushed garlic into the meat, making sure to get plenty down into the slits. Place the meat in a roasting pan. Place the pan in the oven, and roast for 10 to 15 minutes, until the garlic and fat on the roast begin to brown.

Remove the meat from the oven, and reduce the oven temperature to 350 degrees. Cover the meat loosely with foil, and return to the oven. Roast for 2 hours.

While the meat is roasting, prepare the mint sauce. Place the mint leaves in a bowl, and cover them with boiling water, salt, vinegar, and sugar. Stir well, and let cool.

When the lamb has roasted for 2 hours, remove the foil. Increase the oven temperature to 400 degrees, and cook 10 minutes more, or until the garlic and fat on the roast are a rich golden brown. Do not overcook. I prefer lamb to be rare to medium-rare so that the middle of the roast is light pink when carved. Serve the lamb with the mint sauce.

Makes 4 to 6 servings.

Boiled Beef with Biscuits

This easy-to-make recipe was always one of my mother's favorites. Typically, she would cook it all day and serve it for dinner, but it can also be cooked overnight. It may be cooked in a slow cooker on medium or, as Mom usually did, in a conventional oven. It wasn't uncommon for her to use venison instead of beef, but it's delicious with either!

1 (2 ½- to 3-pound) beef or venison roast
Salt and black pepper
16 ounces beef broth, regular or low-sodium
2 cups water

¼ cup finely chopped sweet onion (like Walla Walla, Vidalia, or Texas Sweet)
2 garlic cloves, crushed
1 recipe of June's Southern-Style Biscuits (page 2)

If using a conventional oven, preheat the oven to 275 degrees.

Place the roast on a work surface, and generously sprinkle with salt and black pepper. Pour the broth and water into a large Dutch oven or roasting pan. Place the roast in the pan. Bring to a boil over medium-high heat. Add the onions and garlic. Remove from the heat. If using the conventional-oven method, cover the pan, and cook the beef in the oven for about 8 hours, until the beef falls apart easily when pulled with a fork.

If using a slow cooker, once the broth is brought to a boil on the stovetop and the onions and garlic are added, let cool for a few minutes, and transfer the roast and the liquid to the slow cooker. Cook the roast in the slow cooker on medium for 8 hours or more.

Transfer the beef and all the broth from the pan or slow cooker to a large serving bowl. To serve, crumble the hot biscuits into individual bowls. Ladle the broth on top of the biscuits, and add a generous portion of the boiled beef to each bowl. This dish is always best when biscuits, broth, and beef are fresh and hot.

Makes 6 servings.

Cod Poached in White Wine with Garlic and Capers

Cod is a delicate, yet firm, white fish, perhaps best known for being battered and deep fried. It's also wonderful baked, grilled, or poached, as long as you're careful not to overcook it.

I first remember having this dish while spending a weekend with my mother and Aunt Helen on Cape Cod, just east of Hyannis Port, Massachusetts. I was around eleven, and I recall my father was in New York City recording that week, staying at our apartment there.

I had gone fishing with a local fisherman, a friend of the folks of whom we were guests. I caught three cod that day, bottom fishing with live bait. Cod are scarcer now in those once bountiful waters, but back then, we couldn't keep them off the hook. I came back to the house and proudly presented our catch, which we cleaned and filleted right there in the kitchen.

I remember Mother laughing a lot that day while we spent hours on the beach, walking in the cool sand and gazing out at the sea. It's a wonderful memory, and I think of that day whenever I make this dish.

2 to 3 tablespoons olive oil
3 garlic cloves, crushed
2 tablespoons non-pareil capers, divided
2 large cod fillets, skinned and
   salted on both sides

2 tablespoons chopped fresh Italian parsley
   or 1 teaspoon dried parsley flakes
1 cup dry white wine
1/4 cup heavy cream or half-and-half
Salt and freshly ground black
   pepper to taste
1/2 lemon

In a medium enameled cast-iron or nonstick skillet, heat the olive oil over medium to medium-high heat for 1 minute. Add the garlic and half of the capers, and cook for 1 minute, stirring occasionally. Do not allow the garlic to get too brown or to burn, as that will make it bitter.

Lay the cod fillets on the browning garlic, and continue to cook over medium heat for 1 minute. Turn the fillets over, taking care to avoid damaging the delicate fish, and cook the other side for 1 minute.

Add the remaining capers, parsley, and wine. Increase the heat to medium-high, and cook until the wine begins to boil. Cover the pan, and reduce the heat to medium-low. Simmer the fish for 5 minutes. Carefully remove the fillets to a serving platter.

Return the pan to the heat, and add the cream, shaking the pan gently to blend in the cream. Once heated through, spoon the sauce over the fish, season with salt and black pepper to taste, and squeeze the lemon over the fish just before serving.

Makes 4 servings.

JOHN CARTER'S TIP: Using cream, rather than half-and-half, will make a tastier and heartier dish.

Pan-Fried Trout Fillets

Fish of all types and flavors was always a favorite around the Cash household. We caught a lot of the fish we ate out of Old Hickory Lake, on which our home sat. There were also times when we would catch a stringer full of trout while touring the western states.

One long weekend out West, we decided to float down the McKenzie River in Oregon. We caught a "good few" that sunny, warm day. I'll never forget the method the guides used to prepare our catch on the banks of the river after the float.

Last year I took my wife, Ana Cristina, and my children, Jack, Joseph, and AnnaBelle, to the McKenzie River and floated it again. We were with a different guide service, but the shore-side method of fish preparation was the same. While my father's favorite way to prepare fish was deep frying, I'm a big fan of this pan-fried trout.

2 large eggs, beaten well
½ cup whole milk
Salt and black pepper
Dash of cayenne pepper, optional

1 (20-ounce) box pancake and waffle
    mix (like Krusteaze or Bisquick)
8 medium-size rainbow trout, skinned,
    filleted, and cut as small as 1-inch chunks
1 cup (2 sticks) butter, for frying

Pour the eggs and milk into a zip-top plastic bag. Add the salt, black pepper, and cayenne pepper, if using. Put the pancake mix in a second zip-top plastic bag.

Place the trout in the bag with the egg mixture, and shake well. Remove from the bag, and place in the bag with the pancake mix, leaving plenty of air in the bag before zipping it closed. Shake the bag until the fish is well covered with the pancake mix.

Heat the butter in a large skillet over medium heat until bubbling. Carefully place the fish pieces in the pan one at a time until the pan is full, not overfilling the skillet. Cook until the fish is golden brown, 4 to 5 minutes. Carefully turn the fish over, and cook the other side until golden brown, another 4 to 5 minutes. Remove the fish from the skillet, and place on a paper towel–lined plate to drain. Serve with Cash's Spicy Tartar Sauce (page 70) and lemon slices.

Makes 6 to 8 servings.

John and June's Cashburgers

These veggie burgers were invented by my parents in October of 1995. They got all the ingredients from the 4 Seasons Health Food store in Hendersonville, Tennessee, where we lived.

2 cups cooked brown rice (my parents used Seven Kinds brand) or you can use any combination of whole grains (such as rice, rye, barley, millet, red bulgar wheat, quinoa, wild rice)

2 cups chickpeas or soybeans, cooked and drained (you can use canned)

1 tablespoon roasted sunflower seeds, optional

¼ cup roasted chestnuts, peeled and chopped, optional

2 tablespoons (or more) olive oil

1 medium onion, diced

¼ cup chopped fresh okra, optional

2 carrots, shredded

1 bell pepper, chopped

1 medium potato, diced

¼ cup diced fresh squash

8 to 10 mushrooms, diced, optional

½ cup fresh or frozen corn kernels

¼ cup tapioca flour or almond flour

1 to 2 teaspoons salt

2 teaspoons freshly ground black pepper

1 teaspoon garlic flakes

1 teaspoon sugar or raw or regular honey

Olive oil or safflower oil, for frying

Place the rice (or grains) and chickpeas in a large bowl. Mash them together with a fork to form a thick paste-like mixture. Stir in the sunflower seeds and chestnuts, if using.

Heat 2 tablespoons of olive oil in a large skillet or wok over medium-high heat. Add the onion, okra, if using, carrots, bell pepper, potato, squash, mushrooms , and corn, and cook, stirring, until tender. (You may need to cook the vegetables in batches.) Add the vegetables to the rice mixture. Stir in enough tapioca flour to bind the mixture together, about ¼ cup. Stir in the salt, black pepper, garlic flakes, and sugar. Form the mixture into 6 to 8 patties.

Heat the oil in a large skillet over medium-high heat. Add the vegetable patties, and cook until nicely browned, about 5 to 8 minutes on each side.

Makes 6 to 8 burgers.

John & June's CASHBURGERS

Invented Oct 7 '95

Ingredients: Call from Health Food Store — 4 seasons, (Hinkle)

* Seven kinds of Brown Rice
* Soy Beans
* Roasted Sunflower seed
* Cook grains separately; Boil 45 minutes Until all the Water is cooked out.

Following ingredients hand cut — chopped Roasted Chestnuts — Onions — Okra — Carrots. Bell pepper — Potatos — Squash — Mushrooms Corn.

Lightly stir fry vegetables. Add vegetables and grains together.

TAPIOCA FLOUR: the Cohesive ingredient Stir in as much flour as it takes to hold everything together.

Make into Patties and fry in Olive or Safflour Oil.

Seasoning: Cracked Black Peppercorns Garlic flakes or minced, Salt — Sugar or Honey — to taste.

You can flavour the patties any Way you Want — Oriental — Mexican,

JOHN CARTER'S TIP: I wanted to include my dad's handwritten recipe card for Cashburgers, even though there are no exact amounts listed and no instructions as to how he and my mom actually made the burgers. My recipe tester and I devised a recipe that works with various substitutions and suggestions since some of the original ingredients may be hard to find or are not part of your usual pantry staples.

Tempeh and Vegetable Oriental Stir-Fry

In the 1990s my parents really got into expanding their culinary tastes more toward Asian flavors, eating a lot of fresh vegetables, brown rice, and alternate protein sources. Tempeh, a fermented soy product, has a great flavor and is a tasty replacement for chicken or pork in stir-fry dishes.

1 tablespoon rice wine vinegar

¼ cup soy sauce

½ teaspoon ground ginger or
   1 teaspoon minced fresh ginger

½ teaspoon sesame oil

2 garlic cloves, finely minced

1 tablespoon raw or regular honey

4 to 6 ounces tempeh, diced
   into small cubes

2 tablespoons vegetable or canola oil

2 tablespoons minced shallots

½ cup roasted unsalted cashews

1 green bell pepper, diced

1 cup diced carrots

1 (8-ounce) can sliced water
   chestnuts, drained

1 (8-ounce) can sliced bamboo
   shoots, drained

1 ½ cups chopped broccoli crowns

½ tablespoon all-purpose flour

3 tablespoons water

1 tablespoon hoisin sauce

3 to 4 cups cooked whole-grain brown rice

In a medium bowl combine the vinegar, soy sauce, ginger, sesame oil, garlic, and honey. Stir well, and add the tempeh. Marinate in the refrigerator for 1 hour, and then drain. Reserve the marinade.

In a wok or medium skillet heat the oil over medium-high heat. Add the shallots, and stir-fry until they begin to become translucent, for about 2 minutes.

Add the tempeh to the pan, and stir-fry for several minutes, until it begins to brown. Add the cashews, and stir-fry for another minute. Add the bell pepper, carrots, water chestnuts, bamboo shoots, and broccoli, and continue to stir-fry until the broccoli is wilted but still crunchy, for about 5 minutes.

In a small bowl whisk together the flour and water, and add the mixture to the reserved marinade, stirring until well blended. Add the hoisin sauce. Pour the marinade over the vegetables and tempeh, and continue to stir-fry for another 3 minutes. Serve hot with whole-grain brown rice.

Makes 6 to 8 servings.

Dale Jett's Everything Fried Rice

Dale is the grandson of my great-uncle and great-aunt, A. P. and Sara Carter. He has lived in Hiltons, Virginia, his whole life. His singing voice is reminiscent of his family's music.

He is also an accomplished cook, and he is a master in preparing this easy dinner made with leftover chicken, pork, or steak. This is a welcome all-in-one meal for the whole family. Though peas and carrots are listed below, the list of vegetables that work well in this dish has no end.

3 tablespoons butter, divided

1 teaspoon sesame oil

¼ cup chopped onions

1 to 2 garlic cloves, crushed

2 tablespoons chopped fresh ginger
 or 1 teaspoon ground ginger

⅓ cup chopped carrots

⅓ cup green peas

1 cup cooked chopped meat (steak, chicken, or pork—or a mixture of all three)

2 large eggs, beaten well

2 cups cooked rice

3 tablespoons soy sauce or to taste

Other veggies to add: chopped broccoli, diced sweet peppers, diced celery, green beans (halved), diced fresh jalapeño peppers

Heat 2 tablespoons of the butter and the sesame oil in a wok or deep skillet over medium heat until fully melted and beginning to bubble. Add the onions, garlic, and ginger, and cook until the onions are translucent and the garlic is just beginning to brown.

Add the carrots and cook for 3 minutes, stirring constantly. Add the peas, meat, and eggs, and stir-fry together for another 3 minutes. (If the eggs start to get too brown, turn the heat down a bit.) Add the rice and the remaining 1 tablespoon of butter, stirring the mixture together. Stir-fry for another 3 minutes, and add the soy sauce. Stir-fry for 2 minutes, and then remove from the heat. Serve immediately.

Makes 4 servings.

Ana Cristina Cash's Slow-Roasted White Wine Chicken with Apples

Every family has a favorite dish or at least a most popular one. This is undeniably one of my own family's favorites. A similar recipe has been in my family for a while, but over the past few years, my wife, Ana Cristina, has perfected it, adding in the apples and a few of her own special touches to enhance the dish.

We have a set of stoneware cooking pots and pans, and just a few months ago, my favorite pan broke after I'd used it for over ten years. I searched online for weeks before I found one exactly like it, as the item had been discontinued. You can make this dish even if you don't have a stoneware pan, but there may be variations in cooking time depending on what kind of cooking pan you use. A metal pan, for example, may cook faster than a stoneware baker. Either way, as long as the chicken can be covered with a lid and the chicken itself does not touch the lid while cooking, any pan can work. The chicken must also fit relatively snugly into the pan, as it will rest on the apples as it cooks and should not be able to move off the pieces of fruit.

1 large red apple, cored and cut in quarters, horizontally and evenly
1 whole (4- to 6-pound) roaster chicken, rinsed and patted dry
Salt and black pepper

2 teaspoons paprika
1/2 teaspoon mild chili powder
1/4 teaspoon cayenne pepper, or to taste
2 cups dry white wine
2 garlic cloves, finely chopped

Preheat the oven to 300 degrees.

Place the apple pieces in a stoneware baker or large roasting pan in a single layer, covering the bottom. Sprinkle the chicken generously with salt and pepper, covering the entire bird, as well as the inside. In a small bowl mix the paprika, chili powder, and cayenne pepper together, and coat the outside of the bird evenly with the spice mixture.

Pour the white wine into the pan until it almost covers the apples, about 2 cups. Place the chicken on the apples, breast side up, and cover the pan. Place in the oven, and roast for 2 to 2 1/2 hours, until the chicken is very tender and its juices run clear when pierced with a fork.

Remove the pan from the oven, and increase the temperature to 400 degrees. Remove the cover from the pan, and return the chicken to the oven. Roast it for 15 to 20 minutes, until browned, and then remove from the oven. Spread the garlic on top of the chicken. Place the chicken back in the oven, and cook, uncovered, for 5 minutes. Watch the garlic carefully, as you don't want it to burn and become bitter.

Remove the chicken from the oven, place it on a serving platter, and carve as desired. Serve the chicken while still hot. Make sure to put a portion of the apple on the plate with each chicken serving.

Makes 8 servings.

Grandma Carrie Cash's Buttermilk Fried Chicken

Comfort foods, the same things he ate as a boy, were Dad's all-time favorites. They weren't always the best for his health, but these foods he loved the most were always his first choice. The top of his list was likely to be fried chicken or, should he return after a successful hunt bearing game, a fried squirrel or rabbit.

Grandmother Carrie Cash fed a large family her whole life. She had her own children early on, then came the grandchildren, and later on the great-grandchildren. Cousins and friends would stop by regularly, and there was never a time that there wasn't something good to eat in her kitchen. Gramma had many recipes that she herself created, was heir to, or added her own personal enhancements to.

When I visited on Sundays as a boy, the most common main course was fried chicken. My father loved it extra-extra crispy, and Gramma made the best, in my opinion. I recall her coming to the table, wearing an apron, a little sweat still on her forehead from her hours of effort at the stove. In her hand was a large platter, covered with a red-and-white checkered cloth. She set that platter down on the table, and when the cloth was removed, a generous billow of steam would rise from the delicacy beneath—piece after piece of hot, fresh, crispy, Southern-fried chicken. We all dug in. There was never a single piece or crumb left.

2 (4 1/2-pound) fryer chickens, cut into pieces, breasts split

1/2 teaspoon salt, plus more for seasoning the chicken

1/2 teaspoon black pepper, plus more for seasoning the chicken

1/2 cup buttermilk

1/2 cup whole milk

4 large eggs

4 cups vegetable or peanut oil

1 1/2 cups all-purpose flour

1/2 teaspoon rubbed sage

1/2 teaspoon paprika

1/4 teaspoon cayenne pepper

Place the chicken pieces on a work surface, and sprinkle them generously with salt and black pepper.

Pour the buttermilk and milk into a large bowl. Add the eggs, and beat with a fork or whisk until well mixed. Put the chicken pieces in the milk mixture, and cover. Refrigerate for 2 hours or overnight.

When ready to fry the chicken, heat the oil in a deep fryer or deep cast-iron skillet to 425 degrees.

Put the flour in a large zip-top plastic bag. (I like to use a 2-gallon bag, but 2 single gallon bags are also an option.) Add $1/2$ teaspoon of the salt and $1/2$ teaspoon of the black pepper, and the sage, paprika, and cayenne pepper. Remove the chicken pieces from the milk mixture, and place them in the bag with flour, sealing the bag while leaving air in it. Shake the bag until all the pieces are thoroughly coated with flour.

Remove the chicken pieces from the flour, and place them back in the milk mixture, making sure they are completely wet. Then, put the chicken pieces back in the flour. At this point, you may need to add more flour to ensure the chicken is completely covered.

Carefully place the chicken pieces into the deep fryer or skillet, making sure not to crowd the skillet. Cook the chicken until golden brown, about 15 minutes on each side. Remove the chicken from the skillet with metal tongs, and place on a paper towel–lined platter to drain off excess grease. Serve immediately, while still hot.

Makes 6 to 8 servings.

JOHN CARTER'S TIP: Take care when frying or deep frying. Grease fires can be dangerous. If oil catches on fire, smother the fire with a cookie sheet that is larger in diameter than the skillet.

Fried Rabbit with "Rabbit-Tail" Gravy

My father was an outdoorsman and took me hunting as soon as I could walk. He taught me to shoot with the same .22 rifle that his father had used to teach him to shoot. We seldom went to the woods without bringing back a rabbit or a squirrel. He taught me how to clean and cook them, too, just as his father had taught him. Although this is less common in the world we live in today, I personally cherish these times I had with my dad, in the woods, seeking food to feed our family. Of course, if rabbit isn't available, it can be replaced with chicken pieces.

Fried Rabbit

1 fresh or frozen rabbit, cut into pieces	3/4 cup all-purpose flour
1/4 cup buttermilk	1/4 teaspoon rubbed sage
Pinch of salt	Salt and black pepper
2 large eggs	Garlic salt
1/4 cup milk	3 cups vegetable oil, for deep frying
Dash of Louisiana-style hot sauce, optional	

Gravy

5 tablespoons reserved oil from frying rabbit	1 cup milk
3 tablespoons all-purpose flour	Salt and black pepper to taste

Place the rabbit pieces in a large zip-top plastic bag. Add the buttermilk and a pinch of salt. Refrigerate overnight or for at least 2 hours.

Combine the eggs, milk, and hot sauce, if using, in a large bowl, and whisk or beat with a fork to combine.

Remove the rabbit pieces from the bag and rinse. Place the rabbit pieces in the milk mixture. Put the flour in another large zip-top plastic bag. Add the sage and pinches of salt, black pepper, and garlic salt to the flour. Put the rabbit pieces in the bag of flour, and shake thoroughly. Transfer the rabbit pieces to a plate.

Heat the oil in a deep fryer or deep cast-iron skillet to 400 degrees. Carefully place the rabbit pieces in the hot oil, using long tongs and taking care not to splash the hot grease. Be sure to use a skillet large enough to hold all the rabbit pieces and the grease without boiling over the top. Fry until the rabbit pieces are golden brown, for about 15 minutes. Remove from the heat. Carefully remove the rabbit pieces from the oil, and place on a paper towel–lined plate to drain. Cover the rabbit pieces with more paper towels.

To prepare the gravy, allow the oil in which you cooked the rabbit to cool for 5 minutes. Spoon out 5 tablespoons of the oil to a deep skillet. Reheat the oil over medium-high heat, and add the flour, stirring constantly. Cook until the mixture is a deep brown. Pour in the milk, and bring to a low boil, stirring constantly, until the mixture thickens. Add salt and black pepper to taste and serve with homemade biscuits. The gravy can be poured on the rabbit at the table or served on the side.

Makes 4 to 6 servings.

John Carter's Brunswick Stew

Brunswick stew is an early-American tradition. There is some debate as to where it was invented, with both Georgia and Virginia laying claim. Some say it has German origins, but for many years it was a staple in the southern United States for sure. While recipes vary, traditionally it would have been made with squirrel or rabbit, or whatever meats were available. Beans, vegetables, and tomatoes were usually added.

When I was growing up and hunting with my dad, we would make our Brunswick stew with squirrel and rabbit. These days the meats I use are typically chicken, turkey, or pork—or a combination of all three. I offer up the recipe here as I recall it from childhood. A hearty stew, especially satisfying in the winter months, it is fairly easy to make and a great use for leftover chicken or meats.

2 skinned, cleaned squirrels, heads, offal meats, and tails removed
1 medium-size skinned, cleaned rabbit, head and offal meats removed
1 large baking potato, peeled and cut into chunks
3 garlic cloves, crushed
1 large sweet onion (like Walla Walla, Vidalia, or Texas Sweet), chopped
1 (15-ounce) can lima beans, drained
1 (15-ounce) can yellow corn, drained
1 (15-ounce) can white hominy, drained
1 (15-ounce) can green beans, drained

1 (15-ounce) can chopped tomatoes, drained
1 (10-ounce) can tomatoes and green chilies (like Rotel)
2 cups chicken broth
1 teaspoon dried oregano
1 teaspoon dried basil
1 tablespoon salt or more to taste
2 tablespoons paprika
1 tablespoon mild chili powder
1 teaspoon black pepper
2 jalapeño peppers, finely diced, optional
Cayenne pepper, optional

Place the squirrel and rabbit meat in a large pot, and cover with water. Bring to a boil over medium-high heat. Reduce the heat to low, and simmer, covered, until meat is falling off the bone, about 2 hours. Remove the meat to a large plate, and let it cool. Use two forks to pull the meat apart, removing the bones. Be careful, as small bones are just as dangerous in this dish as when cooking fish. Discard the bones, and return the meat to the pot.

Add the potatoes, and bring to a boil over medium-high heat. Reduce the heat to medium-low, and simmer the meat and potatoes until the potatoes are softened, about 10 minutes. Add the garlic, onion, lima beans, corn, hominy, green beans, tomatoes, and chicken broth. Stir in the oregano, basil, salt, paprika, chili powder, and black pepper. (This is where I often vary my recipe, opting for an even spicier dish by adding the jalapeños and cayenne. It is all up to the cook and the folks who are being fed.) Increase the heat to medium-high, and bring the stew to a boil. Stir well, reduce the heat to low, and simmer, covered, for 30 minutes, stirring occasionally. Serve hot with cornbread or corn chips.

Makes 8 to 10 servings.

JOHN CARTER'S TIP: In place of wild game, use 1 pound of pulled pork or finely chopped baked chicken or roast turkey. You'll need 4 cups of water to cover the pork or poultry, and can skip the 2 hours of cooking called for with the wild game. Add the potatoes, and proceed with the rest of the recipe.

Chapter 4

Travelin' the World

When I was born on March 3, 1970, my father and mother were both at a high point of success in their careers. Dad had a live, weekly television show called *The Johnny Cash Show,* which he produced himself. The show featured all genres of music—from folk and country to bluegrass, choral, gospel, and rhythm and blues. Guests included artists, such as Bob Dylan, Ray Charles, and Bill Monroe alongside Eric Clapton, Loretta Lynn, and James Taylor. Dad saw no division in good music and supported it with all his heart.

They brought me on stage at three weeks old and presented me to their broadcast audience, which was most of the Western Hemisphere. From there they took me on the road with them.

We traveled extensively around the United States and the world when I was a baby. Before I was a year old, I had been to Europe, the Middle East, and Australia. At the time, Dad was one of the most recognized and successful artists worldwide. We were in Germany, France, Ireland, and the United Kingdom at least twice a year. With few exceptions, I was with them on every excursion until I began first grade. Then, when I went to school, I still took off two weeks every spring and fall, bringing my work with me and setting aside time each day for my studies.

Every place we went, my mother would seek out the best food. If it was a small town in Nebraska, we would sometimes eat at the local diner or stop at a fresh produce shop for white corn, crispy and sweet, fresh from a nearby

Top: Outside Bar-B-Que time.

Bottom: On an extended rail trip across Canada circa 1976.

family farm. Or perhaps, while touring by bus through Bordeaux, France, she would halt the driver at a village farmers' market to look through the fresh goat-milk cheeses and cured meats or the varied seafood selections; perhaps there were langoustines still crawling on the ice, or various country patés, whipped with local truffles. No matter our travel destination, fine cuisine was forever in my mother's focus, and she imprinted this on me.

Even at home, there was always an expansive list of ingredients on the grocery list, and from one day to the next, there was no way to know what would be on the menu. It could range from Chinese-style duck with bok choy to German-style schnitzel with spiced red cabbage.

Left: On stage with my father, 1976. My mother and bassist Marshall are in the background.

Above: Microphone foam windscreen boxing, having fun.

Easy Italian Tomato Sauce

Ana Bisceglia worked at my parents' house for years. She had migrated from Naples, Italy, and taught me many delicious southern Italian dishes. Ana often had to cook a quick meal for her family, or my family, for that matter. She taught me this recipe for an easy yet delicious tomato sauce.

3 tablespoons olive oil

4 garlic cloves, crushed, or more to taste

1 (12-ounce) can tomato paste

2 (15-ounce) cans tomato sauce

6 sprigs fresh basil, finely chopped,
  or 1 teaspoon dried basil

Salt and black pepper to taste

Heat the oil in a saucepan (preferably nonstick) over medium heat. Add the garlic, and cook until it begins to brown, being careful not to burn the garlic. (When garlic is overly browned, it gets bitter.) Add the tomato paste, and cook for 3 minutes, stirring often. Fill the tomato paste can with water, and add the water to the pot, stirring until evenly mixed. Return the mixture to a boil. Add the tomato sauce, and stir well. Return to a low boil, and add the basil, and salt and black pepper to taste. Reduce the heat to low, and simmer, covered, for at least 20 minutes, stirring occasionally. The longer you simmer the sauce, the more the ingredients marry and the flavor deepens. The sauce keeps in the refrigerator for at least 1 week.

Makes 5 to 6 cups.

Baked Eggplant Parmesan

This recipe was always one of my favorites. Ana Bisceglia made it weekly for my parents and me. Around our house, pizza wasn't the norm, but this delicious southern Italian dish was.

2 large eggplants unpeeled,
   cut into ¼-inch slices
3 tablespoons salt
1 to 2 cups olive oil
4 large eggs
2 tablespoons milk
1½ cups all-purpose flour

2 cups Easy Italian Tomato Sauce or
   any other fresh tomato sauce
1 (16-ounce) package shredded mozzarella
1 (12-ounce) package fresh
   mozzarella, sliced into rounds
Grated Parmesan cheese

Preheat the oven to 325 degrees.

Place the eggplant slices in a large, deep bowl and sprinkle on the salt. Turn the slices to coat. Cover with water. Press the eggplant down into the water, using plastic wrap or even a plate. Let soak for 30 minutes. Drain off the water and salt mixture. Rinse the eggplant.

Heat the olive oil in a deep skillet over medium heat. Crack the eggs into a large bowl, add the milk, and beat with a fork. Put the flour in a shallow pan. Roll the eggplant in the egg mixture, coating well. Dredge the eggplant in the flour. Place the eggplant in the oil, and cook until golden brown, about 5 minutes on each side. As the eggplant slices brown, place them on a paper towel–lined plate to drain.

Spread a thin layer of the tomato sauce on the bottom of a 9 x 13-inch glass casserole dish. Place a layer of eggplant on the sauce, and cover with more of the sauce. Next, spread the shredded mozzarella over the dish. Add more sauce, followed by another layer of eggplant. Keep repeating in this manner. When near the top of the casserole, finish with a layer of sauce.

Cover with foil. Place the dish in the oven, and bake for 45 minutes. Remove from the oven, and increase the oven temperature to 375 degrees. Remove the foil. Place the fresh mozzarella rounds on top, along with a bit more shredded mozzarella, and finish with a thin sprinkling of Parmesan. Return to the oven, and bake, uncovered, until the top is golden brown and bubbling in the middle. Remove from the oven, and let stand for at least 15 minutes before serving. Serve with extra sauce on the side if desired.

Makes 8 servings.

JOHN CARTER'S TIP: If you want to add vegetables to your lasagna (and we often do at our house), cook chopped zucchini, yellow squash, red bell pepper, and garlic in olive oil, and add a veggie layer along with the layers of sauce, meat, and cheese.

Meat Lasagna

1 pound ground meat (beef, turkey, or wild game)
Salt and black pepper to taste
Oil for greasing the pan
1 (16-ounce) carton ricotta cheese
1 (16-ounce) package shredded mozzarella cheese
1 (12-ounce) package feta cheese
3 cups Easy Italian Tomato Sauce (page 131)
1 (16-ounce) box lasagna noodles, cooked al dente and drained
1 (6-ounce) package sliced provolone cheese
1 (16-ounce) package fresh mozzarella cheese, cut into thin rounds
Grated Parmesan cheese

Place the meat in a large nonstick skillet, and cook over medium-high heat until browned, stirring with a large spoon to crumble. Add salt and black pepper to taste. Remove the meat from the skillet, and place on a paper towel–lined plate to drain.

Preheat the oven to 325 degrees. Oil a 9 x 13-inch glass baking dish. In a large bowl mix together the ricotta, shredded mozzarella, and feta cheese. Spread a thin layer of the tomato sauce on the bottom of the dish. Press a layer of the lasagna noodles into the sauce. Spread another thin layer of the sauce on top of the noodles. Spread a layer of the meat on top of the sauce. Press a layer of the cheese mixture into the meat. Next, add a layer of provolone. Pour more sauce over the top, and then repeat the process, leaving about a 1/4-inch space at the top. The last layer should be tomato sauce.

Cover with foil. Place the dish in the oven, and bake for 40 minutes. Remove the lasagna from the oven, and increase the oven temperature to 400 degrees. Remove the foil, place the fresh mozzarella rounds on top of the lasagna, and sprinkle with the Parmesan cheese. Return the lasagna to the oven, and bake, uncovered, until golden brown. Remove from the oven, and let stand for about 15 minutes before serving.

Makes 8 servings.

John Carter's Seafood Angel-Hair Pasta

3 tablespoons olive oil

3 garlic cloves, crushed

4 large sea scallops

4 large peeled shrimp

6 ounces salmon fillet, cut in cubes
   (or substitute any firm white fish
   such as halibut or grouper)

6 cherrystone clams

1 1/2 cups dry white wine

1/3 cup half-and-half

3 sprigs fresh basil, chopped, or
   1 teaspoon dried basil

Juice of 1 large lemon

16 ounces angel-hair pasta, cooked al dente

Heat the olive oil over medium heat in a deep skillet. Add the garlic, and cook, stirring, until it begins to brown. Add the scallops and shrimp, and cook, stirring, for about 3 minutes on each side. Add the salmon and clams. Pour in the white wine, and cover. Cook until the clamshells pop open. If the clams do not open, increase the heat to medium-high, and bring the mixture to a boil, stirring occasionally and being careful not to break apart the salmon. If any clams do not open within 10 minutes, remove and discard them. Once the clams are open, stir in the half-and-half and basil. Return to a boil briefly, and add the lemon juice. Ladle the sauce and seafood gently over the angel-hair pasta.

Makes 6 to 8 servings.

June's Veal Cutlets with Caper Cream Sauce

My parents had an apartment in New York City, and when I was around ten years old and my dad was recovering from dental surgery, Mom took me out to eat. We went to a little Italian restaurant in Greenwich Village, which we frequented during our visits. One of the dishes I remember having there was a veal piccata made with capers—it was delicious!

At the apartment later that week, while Dad was still recuperating, Mom decided to try her own version of that dish. Over the months that followed, she went through a few variations. She ended up perfecting it into a no-less-mouthwatering dish than the piccata from the Village, but with her own unique touches.

1 pound veal cutlets, sliced thin
Salt and black pepper
2 large eggs
1/4 cup plus 2 tablespoons all-purpose flour, divided
3 tablespoons olive oil
3 garlic cloves, finely chopped

2/3 cup cold water
1 tablespoon capers
1/4 cup white wine
1/2 lemon
8 ounces linguine, cooked al dente, drained, and topped with butter
Parmesan cheese

Place the veal cutlets on a work surface, and sprinkle them with salt and black pepper. Crack the eggs into a wide, shallow bowl, and beat them with a fork. Put 1/4 cup of the flour and a pinch of black pepper in a second shallow bowl.

Heat the olive oil in a large skillet over medium heat. Add the garlic, and cook until it begins to brown. Remove the garlic from the skillet, and reserve for a later use.

Dip the cutlets in the beaten eggs, then dredge in the flour until both sides are lightly covered with flour.

Place the cutlets in the skillet, and cook until nicely browned, for several minutes on each side. Remove the cutlets to a platter.

Combine the water and the remaining 2 tablespoons of flour in a small bowl, and whisk until smooth. Add the capers to the skillet. Stir in the flour mixture, and heat until it boils gently and the sauce begins to thicken. Add the wine, and return to a low boil. Return the cutlets to the skillet, and spoon the sauce over the top. Squeeze the lemon on the cutlets, and serve hot with buttered linguine and Parmesan shaved on the top.

Makes 4 servings.

Weinerschnitzel

My father served in the US Air Force before becoming a professional musician. He was a high-speed Morse code interceptor. Stationed in Landsberg, Germany, Dad listened to the Russian transmissions coming from beyond the Eastern Block. On March 5, 1953, while transcribing a Soviet communiqué, he became the first Westerner to hear the news of Joseph Stalin's death and later received a commendation for it.

During his three-year service in Germany during the Cold War, Dad became well acquainted with the cuisine. One of his lifetime favorite dishes was the world-famous Austrian-style breaded veal cutlet, otherwise known as Weinerschnitzel.

1 pound veal cutlets

Salt and black pepper

¼ cup all-purpose flour

2 large eggs

3 tablespoons milk

1 cup plain fine dried bread crumbs

Vegetable oil for frying

1 lemon, thinly sliced

4 rolled anchovies with capers, optional

Pound the cutlets between 2 sheets of plastic wrap with a meat tenderizer until ¼ inch thick and a roughly round shape. Sprinkle the cutlets with salt and black pepper. Spread the flour on a plate. Combine the eggs and milk in a deep bowl, and beat with a fork. Put the bread crumbs in another deep bowl.

Pour the oil into a deep skillet to a depth of ¼ to ½ inches, and heat over medium-high heat. Dredge the veal cutlets in the flour, and roll them in the egg mixture. Dip them in the bread crumbs, covering them completely but being careful not to press crumbs into the meat. Place the cutlets in the hot oil, and cook until well browned, about 6 minutes on each side.

Place a slice of lemon and a caper-filled anchovy, if using, alongside each serving.

Makes 4 servings.

John Carter's "Magic" Red Cabbage

Good food can be tasty and fun, and cabbage is no exception. I remember eating spiced cabbage on tour with my parents in Germany when I was a boy, and I always enjoyed it with Weinerschnitzel, bratwurst, or roast duck. Years later, I developed my own version of spiced cabbage, recalling my youth. My children love this dish, and I still serve it regularly.

2 tablespoons butter
1/2 tablespoon olive oil
1 medium red cabbage, cored and shredded
2 teaspoons chopped fresh ginger
1/2 teaspoon ground cloves

1/2 teaspoon ground allspice
1/3 cup sugar
1/4 cup balsamic vinegar
Salt and black pepper to taste

Place the butter and oil in a large saucepan, and heat it over medium heat until it's bubbling. Add the cabbage, and cook, stirring constantly, until it begins to wilt. Add the ginger, cloves, allspice, sugar, and vinegar, cover, and cook 10 minutes, stirring occasionally. Remove the cover, reduce the heat to medium-low, and cook for about 30 minutes. During the last few minutes, increase the heat to medium, and cook at a steady boil, stirring constantly, until most of the liquid evaporates. Season the cabbage with salt and black pepper to taste. Remove the cabbage from the heat, and let stand for 5 minutes before serving.

Makes 6 to 8 servings.

Spanish Seafood and Chicken Paella

1 (5- to 7-pound) roaster
   chicken, cut into pieces

1 1/2 teaspoons kosher salt, divided

1/2 teaspoon black pepper

1 tablespoon dried oregano

1 tablespoon paprika (use hot paprika
   if you prefer an extra kick)

2 tablespoons olive oil

1/4 cup chopped Spanish chorizo

1 Spanish or white onion, finely chopped

5 garlic cloves, finely chopped

1/4 cup diced red bell pepper

1/4 cup diced green bell pepper

1 small bunch Italian parsley,
   chopped, divided

4 cups Arborio or Calasparra paella rice

2 tablespoons salted butter

6 cups water

1 (16-ounce) can diced tomatoes, drained

1/4 cup green peas

Pinch of Spanish saffron

6 littleneck clams

6 mussels

8 ounces fresh shrimp, heads on or
   headless, deveined, and peeled

2 cold-water lobster tails, removed
   from shell and deveined

8 ounces sliced calamari

Place the chicken pieces in a large bowl. In a separate small bowl, mix together 1/2 teaspoon of the salt and the black pepper, oregano, and paprika. Rub the spices all over the chicken. Cover and refrigerate for at least 1 hour or overnight.

Place the oil in a large paella pan or large oven-safe skillet. Heat the oil over medium-high heat. Add the chorizo, and cook, stirring, until it begins to brown, for about 2 minutes. Remove the chorizo from the pan, and set aside.

Add the chicken to the pan, and cook, turning often with metal tongs or a metal spatula, until browned. (Careful, as the skin will try and stick to the pan.) Remove the chicken from the pan, and set aside with the chorizo. The chicken meat may be removed from the bone, but I leave it on for extra flavor.

Add the onion, garlic, bell peppers, and about three-quarters of the parsley to the pan, and cook, stirring, just until the onion turns translucent, making sure not to overly brown the garlic, for 2 to 3 minutes. Add the rice to the mixture, and cook, stirring, until the rice begins to brown, about 1 minute.

Stir in the butter. Reduce the heat to medium, pour in the water, and add the tomatoes

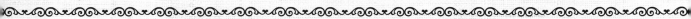

and the peas, stirring well. Cook until the rice absorbs the water, occasionally shifting the skillet around on the burner, allowing the rice to cook evenly for 8 to 10 minutes.

Stir the saffron into the pan. Add the clams and mussels, pushing them into the rice. Then add the chicken and chorizo. Stir again. If you're using headless shrimp and have deveined and peeled them, push them into the rice at this time; if not, keep them to the side. Either way, it's time to shake the pan well, then don't stir it again throughout the rest of the process. (Note that any of the seafood you press into the dish should be added evenly around the dish, not all in one spot.) Reduce the heat to low, and simmer for 8 minutes.

Push the lobster and calamari into the mixture. Also, if you have chosen to use whole shrimp, lay them in a circular pattern around the pan, with the heads facing out, like a clock. At this point, the rice will still be a little crunchy in the middle, but softening on the outside and absorbing the juices in the pan. Cook another 8 to 10 minutes, letting the rice fill the pan and consume all the liquid.

To finish it all off, increase the heat to high, and allow the rice at the bottom of the pan to brown for 1 minute. Then immediately remove the pan from the heat. Sprinkle the remaining 1 teaspoon of salt over the entire dish before serving hot. Garnish with the remaining parsley.

Makes 8 servings.

JOHN CARTER'S TIP: The flavor of the whole is more than the sum of the ingredients in this dish. Part of the chef's magic! I will say that saffron is strong stuff. I am quite sparing with the amount I use because it can quickly overwhelm the dish, and it's quite expensive. I admit, however, its flavor is essential to making an authentic paella.

Cuban-Style Slow-Cooked Beef (Vaca Frita)

I grew up eating a variation of this dish at my parents' table in Jamaica. My mother-in-law, Teresita Alvarez, a talented chef, cooked this dish for me to enjoy again years later on her first visit to Tennessee to see my wife, Ana Cristina, and me. Born in Cuba, Teresita was taught to cook this exquisitely flavored yet common main course as a young girl in her home in Cuba, before migrating to the United States in the 1960s.

1 (2-pound) beef roast
Salt and black pepper
Water
4 garlic cloves, crushed

Juice of 1 large lemon
3 tablespoons vegetable oil
1 medium Spanish or yellow onion,
   cut into slices

Preheat the oven to 300 degrees. Place the roast on a work surface, and sprinkle generously with salt and pepper. Place the roast in a roasting pan, and add water to a depth of 1/2 inch. Rub the crushed garlic cloves into the roast. Cover the pan, and place it in the oven. Roast the beef for 2 hours.

Reduce the oven temperature to 275 degrees, and cook the roast for another 4 hours, or until it is falling apart. Add a little more water if needed along the way. Do not allow the roast to dry in the pan. Remove the roast from the oven, and let cool.

Place the roast in a large bowl, and shred into pieces. Pour the lemon juice over the meat. Cover and refrigerate the meat for at least 4 hours or overnight.

Remove the meat from the refrigerator. In a large, deep skillet heat 3 tablespoons of vegetable oil over medium heat. Add the meat, and cook until it begins to brown. Add the onion, stirring and frying, until the meat and onions are beginning to crisp. Serve hot.

Makes 4 servings.

John Carter's Jamaican-Style Baked and Stuffed Venison Burgers

2 pounds ground venison (or substitute
   very lean ground beef)
1 tablespoon pure cane sugar or white sugar
1/2 teaspoon ground allspice
1/2 teaspoon ground ginger
1/2 teaspoon garlic powder
1/2 teaspoon black pepper
3 tablespoons soy sauce
1/4 cup fine dried bread crumbs
1 large egg, beaten well

1/2 Scotch bonnet or jalapeño pepper,
   finely chopped, optional
1/2 teaspoon Jamaican Jerk
   seasoning, optional
Cooking spray
2 apples, cored but not peeled, cut
   horizontally into 1/2-inch slices,
   roughly 4 slices per apple
Sliced sharp white Cheddar cheese,
   torn into small pieces
8 hamburger buns, toasted

Preheat the oven to 375 degrees.

In a large bowl, combine the meat, sugar, allspice, ginger, garlic powder, black pepper, soy sauce, bread crumbs, and egg. Mix well with a fork or with your hands. For traditional Jamaican flavor, add the hot pepper and jerk seasoning at the end, and blend well with a fork.

Pat out burger patties to 1 inch thick and 4 inches wide. (Wear rubber gloves if you have added the Scotch bonnet pepper to the mixture.) Use your thumb to press an indentation into each, creating a small "bowl" in each burger.

Coat 2 cast-iron or other oven-safe skillets with cooking spray. Place the apple slices flat in each pan, 4 per skillet. Place the burger patties on top of the apple slices, and place a little mound of cheese in each burger "bowl." Place in the oven, and cook, uncovered, for 25 minutes, or until the cheese is browned. Remove and serve on buns with desired accompaniments.

Makes 8 burgers.

JOHN CARTER'S TIP: Wear rubber gloves when handling the Scotch bonnet or jalapeño pepper, and wash your hands thoroughly with soap after chopping it. Be careful not to touch eyes or face. The Scotch bonnet will make this dish extremely hot, and I recommended it for the experienced palate only. If the pepper is excluded, the jerk seasoning itself is sometimes a bit spicy. To make a mild version or these burgers, omit the pepper and the jerk seasoning.

Caribbean Fried Plantains

Plantains are in the banana family, and when I was young they were everyday fare on our table at our home, Cinnamon Hill, in Jamaica. You can prepare this delicious fruit in a variety of ways, but my parents enjoyed them fried, served with mango chutney or garlic aioli sauce.

3 large plantains, still green,
but beginning to soften

$\frac{1}{2}$ cup vegetable oil
Salt

Cut the plantains into $\frac{1}{2}$-inch-thick slices. Place the oil in a large nonstick skillet, and heat over medium-high heat. Add the plantains, and fry on each side until beginning to brown. Remove from the oil, and pat dry with paper towels. Press each piece with a mallet—or your hand, if the plantain is not too hot—to flatten the fruit. Increase the heat to medium-high, return the plantains to the pan, and fry a second time, until the mashed plantains are crispy and brown. Remove from the oil, and pat dry with a paper towel. Sprinkle with a pinch of salt before serving.

Makes 4 servings.

Cinnamon Hill Jamaican Peas and Rice

My parents' home in Jamaica overlooked the Caribbean Sea. An English limestone manor built in 1937 called Cinnamon Hill, it was one of their favorite places on the planet. They spent a third of the year on the road and a third in Tennessee. They spent the rest of the year largely in Jamaica. They loved the flavors of this tropical island nation and its people, climate, and culture. My father loved to snorkel, and he even learned to scuba dive with me when I was a teenager. The table fare in Jamaica is legendary, and one of the most treasured signature dishes from this unique region is Jamaican Peas and Rice. The "pea" used in the Cinnamon Hill kitchen was actually a bean, a red kidney bean (though pigeon peas are used in some places). This is the flavor and culture of Jamaica.

1 1/4 cups dried red kidney beans,
    soaked overnight in water
3 garlic cloves, crushed

1 1/2 cups long-grain white rice
Salt and black pepper to taste
1/4 cup chopped green onions or chives

Drain the soaked beans. Place the beans and garlic in a large saucepan with enough water to cover them. Bring to a boil over medium-high heat. Reduce the heat to low, and simmer, covered, until the beans are tender and easily crush apart between thumb and finger, for about 1 1/2 hours.

Add the rice to the beans, and continue simmering, covered, until the rice absorbs the water, for about 20 minutes. Add salt and black pepper to taste. Serve with the green onions or chives and Jamaican Scotch Bonnet Hot Pepper Sauce. (Recipe on page 65.)

Makes 6 to 8 servings.

Crunchy Mexican Tostada Casserole

Mexican flavors have long been a part of the palate of the United States, and it was no different in the Cash home. My mother had a few favorite Mexican dishes, most of which she would be able to order at a restaurant. This one, however, with the toasted tostada top, was one of her own creation, and I have never seen it on a menu.

1 pound ground beef (we use
    venison in my home)
3 tablespoons mild chili powder
1 tablespoon paprika
1 teaspoon ground cumin
1/2 yellow onion, diced
Pinch of salt
3 garlic cloves, diced
1 cup tomato sauce
Cooking spray

1 (22-count) package crispy corn tostadas
16 ounces shredded mild Cheddar cheese
1/2 cup canned black beans
Handful of fresh cilantro, chopped
1/2 cup diced fresh tomatoes
1/2 cup of your favorite fire-roasted salsa
1/2 cup Zesty and Spicy Chipotle
    Guacamole (page 45)
1/4 cup sour cream

Preheat the oven to 350 degrees.

Place the ground beef in a medium skillet, and cook over medium heat until browned, breaking up the meat with a large spoon. Drain off the grease. Return the skillet to the heat, and add the chili powder, paprika, cumin, onions, a pinch of salt, and garlic. Cook until the onions become translucent, around 3 minutes. Add the tomato sauce. Increase the heat to medium-high, and bring the mixture to a boil, stirring well. Remove the skillet from the heat.

Coat a 9 x 13-inch glass baking dish with cooking spray (not olive oil–based, as olive oil burns easily), and place the tostadas on the bottom of the pan until covered. Add a layer of the ground beef mixture, and cover with half of the cheese. Add a thin layer of black beans on top of the shredded cheese, and another layer of tostadas. Cover with the final layer of ground beef. Cover and bake for 30 minutes. Increase the oven temperature to 375 degrees, and add a final layer of tostadas, topping with the remaining cheese. Bake for 7 to 9 minutes, until the cheese and tostadas begin to brown. Top with the cilantro, and serve hot with the tomatoes, salsa, guacamole, and sour cream on the side.

Makes 8 to 10 servings.

CHAPTER 5

Memories from Friends of the Family

Lunch with Loretta Lynn at the Cash-Carter Home, Late 1970

Loretta Lynn was a dear friend of my parents. She is a unique and brilliant person and a great deal like my parents in so many ways. I've had the chance to produce quite a lot of music for Loretta, and my bond with her has grown over the past decade. She holds a special place in my heart. When I sit next to

Loretta Lynn and Mom in the 1970s.

Courtesy of Loretta Lynn and Patsy Lynn Russell.

Backstage with Loretta at a show during the early '60s.

Courtesy of Loretta Lynn and Patsy Lynn Russell.

her as she records, I look up to her at times, hearing her voice, experiencing her sweet nature, and I feel for sure I see my own mother there again beside me, like the years since her passing have been but the blink of an eye.

I recently had the chance to ask Loretta about her personal visits to my parents' home through the years.

"I remember going to their house in late 1970, when I was a guest on *The Johnny Cash Show*," she recalled fondly. "You were just a baby then!" she said. "I changed your diaper!" She winked.

"Did you have a meal with them?" I asked.

She closed her eyes, remembering the visit. "Well, it was lunch," she said, "and if I recall correctly, we had something I had never had before." Her eyes popped open in delight. "Tomato dumplings! I mean, I grew up eating chicken dumplings, but these were special, with canned tomatoes."

Of course I know this unique dish well! My mother told me she learned to make this tasty Southern meal from her own mother, and that it was a staple food of her youth.

Its preparation begins just as one would prepare chicken dumplings, then it takes a few unexpected turns!

Carter Family Tomato Dumplings

6 cups water for boiling chicken

1 1/2 teaspoons salt, divided

4 (6- to 8-ounce) boneless, skinless
  chicken breasts, cut into 4 pieces each

2 cups all-purpose flour, plus 2 tablespoons
  more for rolling out the dough

1/2 cup vegetable shortening

1 cup water for dumplings

3 tablespoons pure cane
  sugar or white sugar

1/2 teaspoon black pepper, or more to taste

1 (12-ounce) can tomatoes,
  diced and undrained

Dash of cayenne pepper, optional

Place 6 cups of water in a large saucepan, and bring to a boil over medium-high heat. Add 1 teaspoon of the salt and the chicken. Bring to a full boil, and reduce the heat to low. Cover and simmer until the chicken is done and the juices run clear, for about 20 minutes. Remove the chicken from the water. Save the broth. Set the chicken aside to cool. Store the chicken in the refrigerator and save for another use (like June's Walnut and Grape Chicken Salad, page 38).

Sift the flour into a large bowl, add the remaining 1/2 teaspoon of salt, and whisk or stir to blend. Add 1 tablespoon of the shortening to the flour, and using a fork or pastry cutter, blend the shortening evenly into the dough. Add the remaining shortening to the flour, and blend in.

Make a well in the flour mixture, and pour in 1/4 cup of the water, pressing and stirring the water into the flour mixture with a fork or your hand. Continue stirring the remaining 3/4 cups of water into the flour 1/4 cup at a time until the water is completely blended into the dough. If you need more water, add a tablespoon at a time until the dough is soft and pliable.

Cover a cutting board with 2 tablespoons of flour, making sure to cover the entire board. Make sure your hands are dry and covered in flour. Form the dough into a large ball, and dust with flour.

Place the dough ball on the board, and press it flat. Roll out the dough with a floured rolling pin until 1/4- to 1/2-inch thick. Keep adding flour to the board and rolling pin to prevent the dough from sticking. Using a butter knife, cut the dough into 1 x 2-inch strips.

Bring the reserved chicken broth back to a boil, and add the sugar, black pepper, canned tomatoes, and cayenne pepper, if using. Reduce the heat to low, and simmer, covered, for 10 minutes, stirring occasionally. Increase the heat to medium-high, and bring the mixture to a steady boil. Drop the dough strips into the boiling liquid, one at a time. (My mother always said to count to three before adding another dough strip to keep them from sticking together.)

Roll any remaining dough and scraps into a second ball, and roll out and cut more dumplings. Once all the dumplings are in the pot, reduce the heat to low, and simmer, uncovered, for 5 minutes, or until cooked through, carefully stirring only occasionally to make sure the dumplings don't stick to the bottom of the pan. (If you stir too much, the dumplings will fall apart.) Serve immediately.

Makes 4 to 6 servings.

Jane Seymour Remembers Times with Johnny and June

My father and mother were cast as characters on the television show *Dr. Quinn Medicine Woman* during the early 1990s and traveled to Los Angeles for the filming. The star of that successful show was the beautiful and talented Jane Seymour.

Years before, Jane had starred, along with Christopher Reeve, in one of my mother's favorite films, *Somewhere in Time*. Mom loved that tragic romance and was excited to meet one of the stars of the movie. When my parents met Jane on the LA TV set, they immediately struck up a friendship with her and her actor-director husband at the time, James Keach.

Throughout their filming of that first episode, they got to know Jane better and better. I recently talked to Jane about some of her fond memories of my parents. She remembered my dad's character as "always easygoing, fun to be around, and happy, no matter the circumstance."

Jane recalled, "It was late one night, and the scene we were filming was taking forever. But your dad was unfaltering. He had a guitar and sat off to the side of the set playing and singing for the crew and other performers while the cameras were being rearranged for the next scene. I remember he was laughing and talkative."

My parents' friendship with Jane grew closer and closer. Jane remembers my mother as having "divine taste" and that every meal, no matter the occasion, was always formal.

"Limoges china and Wedgwood crystal were always the norm at June's table, a daily affair," she said. "The ladies who worked for her ironed her linens and made sure all was set and formal. There always seemed to be buckets of flowers around, and she would create her own fresh cut arrangements when she had the time. Once, on the day of her release party for her album *Press On*, we put flowers in her silver teapots, crystal decanters, and vases. I will never forget that day!"

Jane inhaled deeply, fondly recalling her dear friend. "We spent the good part of the day cutting and arranging flowers, taking our time to make sure each was cut to the correct length for each particular display," she said.

Jane described my mother's favorite color, a unique tone of sky blue. Mom had created the color herself with the painters for our home in Hendersonville, and most of her arrangements were centered around that particular hue.

Jane remembered, "The blue was everywhere at her table: Her tablecloth, the napkins. Even the crystal glasses were a shade of light blue. Every time I look at the sky, I am reminded of your mother."

Jane spent a good deal of time with my parents at Cinnamon Hill, our home in Rose Hall, Jamaica. "The food there was always special, and your mom had her favorite dishes," she recalled. "The cooks there, with inspiration from your mom, created unique dishes, which I always liked."

One dish Jane particularly enjoyed from my parents' Jamaican table was Cheese Chicken. The Jamaican chickens were always free range, and the cook at the house bought them directly from the butcher. It's a simple dish with its own distinctive traits.

Above: Dad and Mom with Jane at the Jamaican home.

Left: Jane with husband at the time James Keach, sons Johnny and Kris, and Mom and Dad.

Jamaican Cheese Chicken

In Jamaica, we used New Zealand white Cheddar, as it was readily available at the markets. If you can find it, I recommend using it. If not, any other white Cheddar is fine.

2 cups vegetable or peanut oil
1 (3- to 4-pound) free-range, organic-fed
    whole chicken, cut into pieces for frying

Salt and black pepper to taste
8 ounces shredded sharp white Cheddar
    cheese

Preheat the oven to 400 degrees. Place the oil in a deep cast-iron skillet or deep fryer, and heat to 375 degrees. Using tongs, carefully put the chicken pieces in the oil. (Unique to this dish, there is no breading.) Fry the chicken until golden brown, maintaining the oil temperature at about 325 degrees (its temperature will drop when you first add the chicken). Remove the chicken, drain off the oil, and pat the chicken dry with paper towels. Sprinkle the chicken with salt and black pepper to taste.

Place the chicken on a broiler pan, and cover each piece generously with the cheese. Place the chicken in the oven, and bake for about 20 minutes, or until the cheese begins to brown. Remove from the oven, and serve immediately.

Makes 6 to 8 servings.

Billy Bob Thornton Recalls Breakfast with the Cash Family

Academy Award–winning actor Billy Bob Thornton was a friend of my mother and father and was close with them during the time he was married to Angelina Jolie. Billy Bob remembers fondly the times he spent with my parents and one of the unforgettable experiences he had at their table.

"Your dad was the one who seemed to be larger than life to me. I was always nervous around your dad," he said.

"I was friends with Willie Nelson—and he was always easy to talk to. I was also close with Waylon Jennings and Kris Kristofferson, and we had a lot of fun in the old days. They seemed accessible and easy to be around, though I didn't feel very smart around Kris, since he was a Rhodes Scholar and all. But your dad? I felt like the very air around him had power. He was intense."

Once, when Billy Bob was in town recording music with master musician Marty Stuart, Dad invited him to stay at the house for a few days.

Billy Bob said he was uncomfortable with this. "I told your dad that if I wake in the night, sometimes I wander to the refrigerator and see what leftovers I might find. I wouldn't know what to do if I encountered Johnny Cash half asleep at the refrigerator!"

My father answered in his deep, rich voice, "Well, as long as you aren't in your drawers, it would be just fine."

Billy Bob and Angelina didn't wind up staying at the house during that particular visit, but they did come over for breakfast.

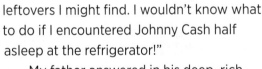

From left: Rosanne Cash, Billy Bob Thornton, Tiffany Lowe, Mom, and Dad.

"I have the worst food allergies in the world," Billy Bob told me. "I went to your mom's house for breakfast that day, and we sat down to a feast. Of course, most all of the items on the table were things I couldn't eat. There were scrambled eggs with cheese, country sausage gravy, biscuits, and hash brown casserole. I sat and talked to your dad while the food was served and was too nervous to tell him that if I ate these things, I might get sick. Instead, while he wasn't looking, I pushed the items around on the plate, to make it look as if I was eating. He would look away, and I would shift the eggs where the biscuit was, cut up things, but not take a bite."

But my father couldn't be fooled. The Man in Black, larger than life, looked at Billy Bob, his eyes narrowed and intense. "I know what you're doing. Please eat your breakfast."

Dutifully, Billy Bob began to eat. Bite after bite. The food was wonderful, but he knew there would be a high price to pay for the dangerous feast.

My mom turned away from her chat with Angelina and turned to my dad and Billy Bob.

"Billy, do you like the eggs, biscuits, and gravy?" she asked.

"Why, yes, ma'am," Billy Bob replied, nervously glancing at my father. "I love them, but I sort of get a stomachache when I eat wheat, eggs, and meat . . . sometimes," he stammered, trying to minimize the fact.

My mom smiled at him. "Why, try this salad! It's my special recipe."

She handed him the faux crystal serving dish, filled with fresh vegetables.

"This is from last night," she said. "But I put it on the table for you to try. Johnny won't eat it as it's loaded with cucumbers. He hates cucumbers. But I love it, and I really think it's better the second day, after being refrigerated overnight."

Billy Bob was grateful to take a heaping spoonful of that unique veggie salad of my mother's creation.

Kris Kristofferson and Dad at Kris's doctorate in the 1970s.

June's Vegan Avocado, Tomato, and Onion Salad

3 large tomatoes, seeds removed
    and cut into small cubes
½ large sweet onion (like Walla Walla,
    Vidalia, or Texas Sweet), diced
1 medium cucumber, peeled and diced
2 ripe, semi-soft avocados, peeled and diced

3 sprigs fresh basil, chopped, or
    1 teaspoon dried basil
Up to ¼ cup sugar (to taste), optional
Several big pinches of salt and black pepper,
    or to taste

Combine the tomatoes, onions, cucumber, avocado, and basil in a large bowl. Add the sugar, if using, and the salt and black pepper. Stir together until well blended. Refrigerate for at least 1 hour, and stir again before serving. My mother liked this dish sweet, but the sugar is optional.

Makes 1½ to 2 cups.

John Prine Recalls the Fate of a Bowl of Johnny's Old Iron-Pot Chili

My father and John Prine were close friends for years. John is one of America's greatest living songwriters, a funny and kind man who, through his entire life, has been a lover of fine food.

Shortly before I started writing this book, I had the honor of speaking to him. He fondly recalled his love for my father and how he missed his jokes and camaraderie. When I asked him about his memories of my dad's cooking, he immediately chuckled and recounted a memorable tale.

For years, John had a party on his birthday. It was always a fantastic festival of music and food where loved ones, family, and friends celebrated creativity and life's journey. The first time John invited my father to his birthday party, it was early in their friendship. Dad couldn't attend the party, but he had their mutual friend, David Ferguson, take John a very unique birthday gift.

This special hot and steaming gift was inside a tightly wrapped plastic bowl. Once David made it to the party and handed the birthday boy the bowl, John noticed there was a letter attached. He peeled open the letter, which smelled of chili powder and raw onions.

John told me that as he pried the cover open, the glorious scent of chili powder and spices wafted teasingly up to this nose. He slipped his finger in the bowl and got a little chili on it. He smacked off the still-hot stew and was almost overwhelmed by its flavor.

"This wasn't just any chili!" he exclaimed. "This was a veritable taste sensation, no denying it!"

But as fate would have it, John never got the chance to finish that first bowl of my father's chili. Someone called his name just as he was sampling that first bit, and he quickly put it in the refrigerator, pushing it way to the back, hoping it would go unnoticed until he could come back to eat up later.

But as parties usually go, nothing in the refrigerator was safe! John found himself tending to his guests all through the night, and sometime during the evening's festivities, or maybe even in the early morning hours, someone got ahold of that bowl—tucked far behind the milk, watermelon slices, beer cans, and potato salad.

When John found the remnants the next morning, all that was left was the empty bowl in the sink, tossed among numerous dirty dishes and glasses, with only a few beans, a scattering of ground meat, and the lingering scent of the delicious chili to mark what once was. My father's handwritten note had fallen to the floor.

In the years that followed, John went on to eat a few bowls of my father's chili and remembers it as being his all-time favorite chili. But he still regrets missing out on that very first bowl!

Dad always said he would never give up his recipe, but when my grandmother Carrie asked him for it, he relented. I was there when he gave it to my dear grandmother, and I remember what he said when he handed it to her: "I guarantee I use this recipe. I start with it, anyway. . . . Then from there, each and every time, I go a slightly different direction." Something tells me certain secrets were omitted!

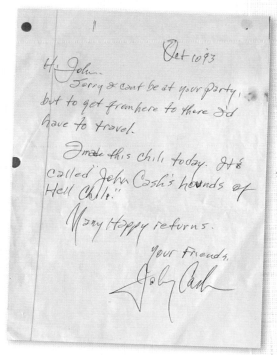

Bottom line, Dad felt that the most important ingredient in chili was creativity, and he never made two batches just alike. Neither do I. I offer a blueprint here, with my own touches added in.

Johnny Cash's Iron-Pot Chili with a Roasted Top

1 pound ground venison or ground beef

1 pound ground turkey

2 tablespoons olive oil

4 garlic cloves, crushed, divided

1 1/4 large sweet onions (like Walla Walla, Vidalia, or Texas Sweet), diced

1/2 pound venison backstrap or sirloin steak, cut into small chunks

1 (16-ounce) can diced tomatoes

1 (12-ounce) can tomatoes and green chilies (like Ro-Tel)

1 (12-ounce) can or bottle beer (I prefer a lager or pale ale)

1 green bell pepper, finely diced

1 red bell pepper, finely diced

1 poblano pepper, finely diced

2 jalapeño peppers, finely diced, optional

1 habanero pepper, finely diced, optional

1 tablespoon garlic powder

Pinch of ground cloves

1 teaspoon rubbed sage

1/2 teaspoon dried thyme

1 teaspoon dried oregano

1 teaspoon black pepper

3/4 cup mild chili powder

1/2 cup ground cumin

2 (1 1/2-ounce) packages chili seasoning (like McCormick)

2 (15-ounce) cans pinto beans, drained

2 (15-ounce) cans red kidney beans, drained

1 (15-ounce) can black beans, drained

1 (15-ounce) can great northern beans, drained

1/4 cup raw or regular honey

1/4 cup firmly packed brown sugar

1/4 teaspoon cayenne pepper, or to taste

1 cup water

1/4 cup yellow cornmeal or cornmeal mix (I use cornmeal mix, which contains a bit of flour and baking soda, but if you can't find the mix, plain cornmeal will work just fine)

1 cup crushed corn chips (like Fritos)

1 cup shredded mild Cheddar cheese

Place the ground venison or beef and the ground turkey in a large pot. Cook it over medium heat until browned, using a large spoon to crumble the meat. Remove the meat from the pot with a slotted spoon, and place on a paper towel–lined plate to drain.

Add the olive oil to the pot. Add half the crushed garlic, and cook until it begins to brown just a bit, for about 2 minutes. Add the onions and cook, stirring, until they become translucent, for about 3 minutes. Add the steak to the pot, and cook until browned and done throughout, for 4 to 5 minutes. Stir the ground meats back into the pot.

Add the canned tomatoes and tomatoes and green chilies to the pot, and stir well. Add the beer, bell peppers, poblano, and jalapeño and habanero peppers, if using. Add the remaining crushed garlic, garlic powder, cloves, sage, thyme, oregano, black pepper, chili powder, cumin, and chili seasoning, and stir well. Pour in the pinto beans, red kidney beans, black beans, and great northern beans. Add the honey, sugar, and cayenne pepper, and taste.

Note: This basic recipe is a good starting place, but if you like, this is where your creativity can enter in earnest. There are unlimited variations of flavor. Dad's chili may have even had more mild chili powder than this, but I typically use just a tad less, for my own personal taste. Experiment as you will. In my opinion, most American palates prefer a milder, sweeter chili. Not so at our house, where we say, "Bring on the spice, bring on the flavor!" When I make my chili, if I want a hot batch and a medium batch (there is no mild), I divide the chili into two batches at this point. After transferring half of the chili to a second pot, the first thing I do is add another $1/4$ cup honey, 1 cayenne pepper, and 1 diced habanero to the hot batch. The sweetness cuts the heat and fills the mouth with divine flavor. The hot batch can get as hot as you like, but if I add more *caliente* ("hot"), I always balance with a tad more sweetness. This, again, is up to your own palate.

Cook either a single batch of medium chili or the two batches (one medium, one hot) over low heat, and simmer, stirring often, for at least 30 minutes. Halfway through the cooking time, stir in the water and cornmeal.

Preheat the oven to 400 degrees, and transfer the chili to one or two Dutch ovens or other oven-safe pots. Mix together the corn chips and cheese, and spread evenly on top of the chili. Place in the oven, and bake for 10 minutes, or until the cheese and corn chips are browned.

Serve hot with desired accompaniments. At our house, we serve our chili with sour cream, more shredded cheese, chopped sweet onions, and hot sauce.

Makes at least 12 servings.

JOHN CARTER'S TIPS: Notice I do not add salt to this recipe. This is because there is salt in the cans of beans and tomatoes. For my taste, there is plenty in the canned items to salt the chili sufficiently. If you use salt-free beans or tomatoes, you may want to add some extra salt, depending on your own taste.

When dicing the habanero pepper, wear gloves or hold the pepper with a paper towel while cutting. It's dangerous, and if you touch your eyes after touching this kind of pepper, it can really cause some pain.

Early-Morning Visit with Lisa and Kris Kristofferson

Lisa Kristofferson is quite a mother. Throughout most of her years with Kris, they have lived in Hana, Hawaii. Lisa was close to my parents, and they all traveled together during the years Dad was active with The Highwaymen, which, along with my dad and Kris, included Willie Nelson and Waylon Jennings.

Lisa recalls how at the end of one long tour, the tour bus pulled up to my parents' house early in the morning.

On tour with the Highwaymen. From left: Waylon Jennings, Jessi Colter, Dad, Mom, Willie Nelson, Annie Nelson, Kris Kristofferson, and Lisa Kristofferson.

"Kris was still asleep," she remembered. "But I was awake with the children. Your mother came out to the bus and called us inside, where the children could play."

"I went to freshen up for a moment, but when I came back to the kitchen, I will never forget, your mother had a special moment with our oldest son, Jesse." Lisa laughed out loud here, the memory coming to heart.

"June had made a huge pot of beef and barley soup that was really delicious. I cooled some off and tried to feed Jesse, but he was squirming and intent on exploring all the wild, wonderful new things in that museum of a house. June laughed and lit a candle in a Santa Claus holder, put it just out of his reach, and proceeded to feed him the entire bowl as he stared at the forbidden flame."

Lisa looked to the side, recalling her friend, all those years earlier. "I learned so much from that moment, and that lesson served me well raising my next four children who came along. Distraction and diversion are way better than a struggle. And my! How a wonderful meal can change everything."

June's Beef and Barley Soup

2 tablespoons vegetable oil
1 pound sirloin steak, cubed
1 1/2 cups chopped carrots
1 medium sweet onion (like Walla Walla,
  Vidalia, or Texas Sweet), finely chopped
2 garlic cloves, diced
Sprig of fresh parsley

Sprinkle of dried thyme
1 cup uncooked barley
1/2 cup frozen green peas
1 teaspoon salt
Black pepper to taste
1 (16-ounce) can beef stock
1 (16-ounce) can tomato sauce

In a medium Dutch oven, heat the oil over medium-high heat. Add the beef, and cook until browned on all sides. Remove the meat from the Dutch oven. Add the carrots, onions, garlic, parsley, and thyme. Reduce the heat to medium, and cook, stirring, for 2 minutes. Add the barley and frozen peas. Continue to cook for 3 minutes. Add the salt and black pepper to taste. Stir in the beef stock and tomato sauce. Increase the heat to medium-high, and bring to a boil, stirring often. Add the beef back in, then reduce the heat to low, and cook, covered, until the beef is tender, stirring occasionally, about 1 hour.

Makes 10 to 12 servings.

Lunch at June's Table with Adam Clayton and Bono of U2

In 1988, while touring extensively for the release of their album *The Joshua Tree*, the rock band U2 spent some time recording at Sun Studios with my father's old friend and music producer Jack Clement. Jack called my dad one day when the band was in Nashville and asked if he and Mom could come by and say hello. Not only could they come by, my parents asked them over for lunch!

U2 bassist Adam Clayton recalls that visit all those years ago and how my parents were kind to a couple of road-weary musicians. Through a fellowship initially established around a table piled with delicious foods, there came a bonding and friendship. It was only a few years later when my father and U2 would go on to create some timeless recordings together.

"I should have gotten used to Bono saying things like, 'We're going to have lunch with Johnny and June Carter Cash today,'" Adam said. "On this particular day, we were making a quick stop on a journey that had started in Los Angeles, much of it on the historical Route 66. From Nashville, we planned to take the scenic Natchez Trace to New Orleans, where we had an appointment with producer Daniel Lanois. Our album *The Joshua Tree* was riding high on the US charts, and Bono and I had decided to drive across the country and experience roots music, region by region.

"We arrived at the end of a road to be met by Johnny, June, and John Carter, as well as Cowboy Jack Clement and recording engineer David Ferguson, and were welcomed into Johnny's house. It was an intimate, eclectic-looking abode, not at all like a Nashville mansion. We were ushered inside where a sumptuous lunch had been prepared and laid

At the Cash family table. From left: Dad, Adam Clayton, Doug Caldwell, "Cowboy" Jack Clement, and Bono..

out on the table. This, Johnny told us, was not for us but was for a cookbook June was working on.

"We toured the house while the food was being photographed. Johnny was generous with his time and told us stories from his life that would be of help to two young men on a mission.

"We eventually returned to the table, where we were joined by John Carter and his friend Doug Caldwell. The table had been reset for our lunch, a more traditional fare of salads, spiced fruit—both peaches and apples—Southern-style yeast rolls, and roast chicken, perfect for men who had supped in simple diners along Route 66.

"It was an insight to be with American royalty in a family environment, a reminder of the family life we left behind or never had. Johnny said a prayer at the beginning and then we ate.

"Fellowship around the table is a tried and tested technique for creating intimacy. Jesus would start with washing his guests' feet. This is in a sense what happens when we gather for a meal.

"We were treated to an intimate experience with the Carter-Cash family and friends, and we were richer for it. We were placed in a position of trust, where Johnny and June allowed us into their family, and their banter back and forth underlined the depth of their relationship and their love for each other. We were humbled and later that afternoon carried on our way to make our appointment in New Orleans."

Menu at the Cash home on the day of Adam and Bono's visit:

June's Greek Salad with Potato Salad
Roast chicken
Tomato Dumplings (page 163)
Cash Family Easy Hash Brown
    Casserole (page 6)
Spiced peaches
Spiced baby apples
Green beans with ham hocks

Homemade yeast rolls
Baked Eggplant Parmesan (page 132)
June Carter Cash's "Stuff" (page 85)
Sweet tea
Ice water
Coffee
Blackberry Cobbler with Vanilla Ice Cream
    (page 187)

Blackberry Cobbler with Vanilla Ice Cream

Filling

1 1/2 tablespoons cornstarch
Cold water
1 pint fresh blackberries, rinsed
1/2 cup pure cane sugar or white sugar
2 tablespoons raw or regular honey

Juice from 1/4 lemon
3/4 teaspoon finely grated lemon rind
1/4 teaspoon ground cinnamon
Dash of ground cloves

Crust

1 cup all-purpose flour
1 1/3 teaspoons baking powder
1/4 teaspoon baking soda
Pinch of salt
10 tablespoons salted butter, melted

2 tablespoons brown sugar
1/4 cup half-and-half
Coarse sugar (like turbinado
    or Sugar in the Raw)

Vanilla ice cream

Preheat the oven to 350 degrees.

To prepare the filling, mix the cornstarch with a little cold water, and press with a fork until it is blended to a consistent paste. In a 9-inch square glass baking pan, combine the blackberries, sugar, honey, lemon juice, lemon rind, cinnamon, and cloves. Gently stir in the cornstarch mixture. Let stand at room temperature for 45 minutes.

To prepare the crust, in a large bowl combine the flour, baking powder, baking soda, and salt. In a small bowl combine the butter and brown sugar. Using a pastry cutter, your hands, or two knives, cut the sugar mixture into the flour mixture until it turns into small crumbles. Once the mixture is crumbly, pack it loosely together and make a well in the middle of the mixture. Pour the half-and-half into the indentation, a little at a time, using a fork to mix it with the flour mixture. The dough will be very thick.

Spoon the dough into about 6 or 7 equal portions. Roll each portion in the palm of your hand to form a loose ball. Press each ball of dough into the berry mixture, leaving a bit of space in between.

Sprinkle the top with coarse sugar. Bake for 30 to 35 minutes.

Serve fresh and hot from the oven with vanilla ice cream.

Makes 4 to 6 servings.

CHAPTER 6

Savin' the Best for Last—
Dessert Recipes to Die For

June's New York-Style Cheesecake with Fresh Berry Compote

My mother was a great fan of cheesecake. I recall being in New York City with her in the 1970s and stopping at our favorite deli for the rich and wonderful cheesecake of her liking. Mom always asked for a strawberry compote to go with it. Since we weren't always in New York, Mom eventually decided to create her own recipe so that she could have it anytime. She taught me to make her all-time favorite dessert in our home kitchen in Hendersonville, Tennessee, and I always preferred it to the one from the master pastry chef at the New York deli!

Cookie Crust

1 cup (2 sticks) unsalted butter, melted, plus more for greasing the pan

3 cups vanilla wafer or graham cracker crumbs

1/3 cup sugar

1 teaspoon lemon juice

1 teaspoon grated orange rind

1 teaspoon vanilla extract

Cheesecake Filling

16 ounces whipped or regular cream cheese

1 cup powdered sugar

1 tablespoon lemon juice

2 tablespoons all-purpose flour

2 large eggs, beaten well

2 egg yolks

1/4 cup heavy cream

1 teaspoon vanilla extract

Topping

Fresh Berry Compote (see Pancakes with Fresh Berry Compote, page 18)

Whipped cream

Preheat the oven to 350 degrees. Butter a 9-inch pie pan.

To prepare the cookie crust, in a large bowl mix together the crumbs, sugar, lemon juice, orange rind, vanilla, and 1 cup of melted butter. Press the crumb mixture evenly into the pan. Place the pan in the oven, and bake the crust for 10 minutes, or until it just begins to brown. Remove the pan from the oven and set aside. Increase the oven temperature to 475 degrees.

To prepare the filling, place the cream cheese in a large bowl. Add the sugar, $1/4$ cup at a time, and blend well. Add the lemon juice, all-purpose flour, beaten whole eggs, egg yolks, heavy cream, and vanilla, and beat with an electric mixer until blended. Spoon the filling into the crust, and smooth the top so that it is even with the top of the crust. Place in the oven, and bake for 8 to 10 minutes. Decrease the oven temperature to 350 degrees, and bake for another 30 minutes, or until a toothpick comes out clean.

Let the cheesecake cool to room temperature, and refrigerate until ready to serve. Always cut with a wet knife, heated with hot water. Serve each slice with a heaping spoonful of Fresh Berry Compote and whipped cream.

Makes 6 to 8 servings.

JOHN CARTER'S TIP: I find using whipped cream cheese is easier, but regular cream cheese is fine if it is whipped with a fork or an electric mixer.

June's Heavenly Hash with Fresh Berry Compote

"No one ever left June's table hungry!" remembers Karen Robin, longtime friend and wife of my parents' manager, Lou Robin.

"Every placemat was linen, every dish was fine china, and every glass was crystal," she continued. "Your mother knew how to throw a dinner—or luncheon or breakfast, for that matter! A dinner was an event at your parents' table. And the food was always special.

"June put many different dishes on the buffet table, directing and consulting with the cooks and kitchen staff as to how many dishes should be served and then adding at least another five. But no matter—at the end of the day, there wasn't much left over."

One of Karen's favorite dishes was my mother's Heavenly Hash, accompanied by her Fresh Berry Compote.

½ cup halved maraschino cherries, plus more whole cherries for garnish
½ cup whipped cream, plus more for topping (Mom used Cool Whip, but you could use canned whipped cream or fresh whipped cream)
1 cup chopped fresh pineapple
½ cup shredded sweetened coconut
1 cup small marshmallows
Shortbread cookies (like Walker's), 2 per serving
Fresh Berry Compote (see Pancakes with Fresh Berry Compote, page 18)

In a large bowl, mix together the cherries, whipped cream, pineapple, coconut, and marshmallows. Refrigerate for at least 1 hour.

Place 2 shortbread cookies on each dessert plate. Cover them with the cherry mixture, and spoon on the Fresh Berry Compote and a bit more whipped cream. Top all with a maraschino cherry.

Makes 4 to 6 servings.

JOHN CARTER'S TIP: If you don't have self-rising flour, substitute a mix of 1 1/2 cups all-purpose flour, 2 1/4 teaspoons baking powder, and 3/4 teaspoon salt.

Gramma Carrie Cash's Banana Bread

As a boy, when I visited my grandparents' home with my father, one thing was always certain: good food! One of my top favorites, often fresh from the oven, its scent filling the whole house, was Gramma Carrie's banana bread.

Good cooks make magic, and my grandmother was a wonderful cook!

Though the ingredients are few and simple, hers is the best banana bread on this planet. That's my opinion, anyway.

Lisa Trice, who worked for our family for decades, learned this recipe from my grandmother and still makes it regularly. She sometimes drops off a few cakes when she has spent a day in the kitchen. Lisa's version takes me back to my childhood, recalling time with my grandmother and reminding me of her kindness and sweet nature.

Banana Bread

Butter for preparing the pan

2 very ripe bananas

2 large eggs, beaten well

1 cup white sugar

¼ cup vegetable oil

2 heaping tablespoons orange marmalade

1 teaspoon vanilla extract

1 ½ cups self-rising flour

Frosting

1 cup powdered sugar

½ teaspoon vanilla extract

½ cup sweetened condensed milk

Preheat the oven to 350 degrees. Butter an 8 x 4-inch or a 9 x 5-inch loaf pan.

To prepare the banana bread, place the bananas in a large bowl, and mash them with a fork. Add the eggs, sugar, vegetable oil, marmalade, and vanilla, and mix well. Sift in the flour, a little at a time, stirring well. Scrape the batter into the pan. Place the pan in the oven, and bake for 50 minutes, or until a wooden toothpick inserted in the center comes out clean.

To prepare the frosting, combine the powdered sugar, vanilla, and milk in a small bowl. Mix well with a whisk or beat with an electric mixer until smooth. Let the bread cool completely, and cover generously with the frosting.

Makes 1 loaf.

Doug Caldwell's Blue Ribbon Carrot Cake

Doug is one of my oldest and dearest friends. He is also the most accomplished baker I know, having won numerous awards and accolades. His Blue Ribbon Carrot Cake is legendary—not only around the Caldwell house and my house, but all over the mid-South. It is one of my all-time favorite desserts. They say "practice makes perfect," and Doug's dedicated years of practice have made this the perfect carrot cake!

Carrot Cake

Butter or oil for preparing pan
2 cups all-purpose flour
2 teaspoons baking powder
2 teaspoons baking soda
2 cups sugar
3 teaspoons ground cinnamon
1/2 to 1 teaspoon salt

4 large eggs, room temperature
1 1/4 cups canola oil
2 teaspoons vanilla extract
1 pound bag baby carrots,
    grated (3 cups grated)
1 cup chopped pecans, optional

Frosting

1/2 cup (1 stick) unsalted butter, softened
8 ounces cream cheese, softened
1 teaspoon vanilla extract

4 cups powdered sugar
1 cup chopped pecans, optional

To prepare the cake, preheat the oven to 350 degrees. Butter or oil two 9-inch cake pans or one 9 x 13-inch cake pan.

In a large bowl combine the flour, baking powder, baking soda, sugar, cinnamon, and salt. Form a well in the center of the mixture, and add the eggs, oil, and vanilla. Using an electric mixer on medium-high speed, beat for 3 minutes, scraping the sides down occasionally. The batter will be thick. Stir in the grated carrots with a wooden spoon, mixing well. Fold the nuts into the batter, if using.

Pour and spread the batter into the pans.

Bake the 9-inch cakes for 30 to 40 minutes. If making a 9 x 13-inch cake, bake for 45 to 55 minutes. The cakes are done when a toothpick inserted in the center comes out clean.

Remove the cakes from the oven, and place on a wire rack to cool for 10 to 15 minutes. Remove the cakes from the pans, and place on the rack to cool completely.

To prepare the frosting, combine the butter, cream cheese, and vanilla in a large bowl. Beat with an electric mixer at medium-high speed until smooth. Gradually add the powdered sugar, and continue beating until the desired spreading consistency is reached. If you are adding nuts, fold them in once the icing is smooth.

For a sheet cake, cover the sides and top with icing (or just the top if you want to keep the cake in its baking pan). If making a two-layer cake, place one layer on a serving plate or cake stand, and spread the icing evenly over the sides and top. Place the second layer on top, and spread the frosting on the top and sides.

Makes 10 to 12 servings.

Olga's Dream Cake: Panetela (Cuban Sponge Cake) with Fresh Natilla Custard

This delicious dessert is really just a simple cake covered with custard. It was one of my wife's family favorites growing up. It was passed down to Ana Cristina from her great-aunt Olga, Ana's grandmother Maria's sister. The natilla, which is used as the filling, is a traditional custard dessert from Spain, the land of Ana's family ancestry before they migrated to Cuba, before finally coming to the United States. Ana still makes this delicious dessert and has added a few flairs to make it her very own. It's called Dream Cake because of the cloud-like texture and its dreamy deliciousness!

Panetela Cake

1/2 cup (1 stick) butter, plus more
    for preparing the pan
2 cups sifted all-purpose flour, plus
    more for dusting the pan
1 cup pure cane sugar or white sugar
2 large eggs, room temperature

2 1/2 teaspoons baking powder
1/4 teaspoon salt
3/4 cup milk, room temperature
1/2 cup half-and-half, room temperature
1 teaspoon vanilla extract

Natilla Custard

3 cups half-and-half
2 (12-ounce) cans evaporated milk
1 (12-ounce) can sweetened condensed milk
1 cinnamon stick
1 lemon peel
5 egg yolks
1/4 cup sugar

1/2 teaspoon salt
5 tablespoons cornstarch
    (Maizena preferred)
1 teaspoon vanilla extract
8 to 16 ounces whipped topping
    (like Cool Whip)
Rainbow sprinkles

To prepare the panetela, preheat the oven to 350 degrees. Butter a 9 x 13-inch glass baking pan and dust with flour.

Melt the butter in a large microwave-safe bowl, and pour in the sugar. Using an electric mixer at medium speed or a fork, beat until creamy. Add the eggs, one at a time, and mix until well blended.

Mix the flour, baking powder, and salt in a separate bowl. Combine the milk and half-and-half in a third bowl.

Add half the flour mixture to the egg mixture, and pour in half the milk mixture. Mix until well blended.

Add the remaining flour mixture and milk mixture, and fold gently until mixed well. Pour the batter evenly into the pan. Bake for 30 to 35 minutes, or until golden brown and a toothpick inserted into the middle of the cake comes out clean. Remove from the oven, and place the pan on a wire rack to cool.

To prepare the natilla, mix the half-and-half, evaporated milk, and condensed milk in a large saucepan on the stove. Add the cinnamon stick and lemon peel to the pan. Heat over medium-high for a few minutes, stirring constantly, until the mixture begins to steam, being careful not to let it boil. If the mixture gets too hot, lower the heat. The point is to release the flavors of the lemon and cinnamon into the milk. You'll smell the perfume of the lemon and cinnamon within 3 to 5 minutes. Carefully remove the cinnamon stick and lemon peel from the pan. Reduce the heat to low, and simmer the milk mixture, stirring occasionally, as you temper the egg mixture as explained below.

Mix the egg yolks, sugar, and salt together very well in a separate large bowl. Add the cornstarch, and mix well. Slowly pour 1/4 cup of the hot milk into the egg mixture to temper the eggs and prevent them from scrambling or cooking. Continue to stir in the hot milk, 1/4 cup at a time, mixing well.

Return the mixture to the saucepan, and cook over low heat for 8 minutes, stirring constantly with a wooden spoon until the mixture is thick and creamy.

Remove the natilla from the heat, and stir in the vanilla. It is always best to put the vanilla in at the end because it gives the natilla a wonderful, strong vanilla flavor. Let cool for a few minutes.

ANA'S NOTE: You could make this into a two-layer cake if you preferred, spreading the batter into two 8-inch round cake pans, and baking for 25 to 30 minutes. Once baked and cooled, remove the layers from the pans. Spread natilla between the layers and also on the top and sides of the top layer before spreading the entire cake with Cool Whip and covering with sprinkles.

Once the cake is cooled completely, use a big spoon or spreader to place the natilla on top of the panetela. Make sure to spread the natilla evenly over the panatela, covering the entire surface; you'll end up with a thick layer of custard over the cake.

Pour the entire tub of whipped topping on top of the natilla, and spread evenly over the cake.

Decorate with lots of rainbow sprinkles. (This is Olga's magic touch.)

Makes 10 to 12 servings.

Banana Praline Cake

My sister Tara is an accomplished cook and the mother of two young men: Aran, twenty-two, and Alex, eighteen. She and her husband, Fred, live in Portland, Oregon; they're kind and openhearted, always giving of themselves in humanitarian efforts. With three men in the house, Tara is forever cooking, and she has shared with me her family's favorite desserts. Banana Praline Cake was also one of my mother's top after-dinner treats for years and years.

Praline Topping

3 tablespoons unsalted butter, plus
    more for preparing the pan

1 cup chopped pecans
1/3 cup honey

Banana Cake

2 ripe bananas, mashed
2 1/2 cups almond flour
1/2 teaspoon sea salt
1/2 teaspoon baking soda
1 teaspoon ground cinnamon

1/4 cup (1/2 stick) butter
1/3 cup honey
2 large eggs
1 teaspoon vanilla extract

Preheat the oven to 350 degrees. Butter a 9-inch square baking pan.

To make the praline topping, place the butter and pecans in a skillet, and heat over medium heat. Cook until the nuts are lightly toasted and fragrant, stirring often. Add the honey, and bring to a gentle boil. Cook for 4 minutes while constantly stirring. Then stop stirring, and continue to cook for 1 minute. Keep a very close watch to make sure the mixture does not burn. Remove the pan from the heat and set aside.

To prepare the cake, mash the bananas in a small bowl with a fork. Place the flour, salt, soda, and cinnamon in a large bowl and whisk to mix well.

Melt the butter in a small saucepan, and remove from heat. Stir in the honey. Blend in the eggs and vanilla. Pour into the flour mixture, and stir until blended. Stir in the mashed bananas. Scrape the batter into the prepared pan, and crumble the praline topping on top. Place the pan in the oven, and bake the cake for 30 to 40 minutes, until a toothpick inserted into the center of the cake comes out clean.

Let cool for 15 minutes before serving.

Makes 9 servings.

Tara's Double Chocolate Raspberry Pavlova

Here's another of my sister Tara's favorite dessert masterpieces.

6 egg whites

11 ounces caster sugar or
  regular white sugar

3 tablespoons cocoa powder
  (Tara uses Belgian)

1 tablespoon good balsamic vinegar

1 3/4 ounces good-quality chocolate (70
  percent cocoa solids), chopped into small
  pieces, plus more chocolate for garnish

2 cups cream, whipped and sweetened
  with 1 tablespoon of caster
  sugar or powdered sugar

3 pints fresh raspberries

Preheat the oven to 350 degrees.

Place the egg whites in a mixing bowl, and using an electric mixer with a whisk attachment, beat at medium-high speed until soft peaks form. Add the sugar, 1 tablespoon at a time, and continue beating until the egg whites become stiff and glossy. Be careful not to over beat as it can start to separate. The mixture is ready once it forms stiff, glossy peaks.

Sift in the cocoa powder. Using a large spoon, gently fold in the vinegar and chopped chocolate. The mixture will have a very light brown shade.

Line 2 large cookie sheets with baking parchment. (I find it helpful to dab a little bit of the pavlova mixture underneath each corner of the paper to help it to stick to the tray.) Place a dinner plate on the middle of each tray, and trace around its edge with a pencil or pen to form a circle. (This will act as a guide and ensure both pavlovas are the same size.) For a taller, more dramatic pavlova, use three smaller plates, instead of two larger plates, to make three layers instead of two.

Flip the paper over so the ink or pencil graphite is touching the tray side as opposed to the pavlova side. You'll still be able to see the line through the paper. Pile the pavlova mixture on each circle, smoothing it out to the edges of the lines you have just drawn. Try to divide the mix equally so both have same volume of mixture. I normally smooth out the mixture, but a pavlova is not supposed to look perfect. Feel free to form a few points and peaks if you want. When cooked they'll crisp up and add a bit more interest visually.

Place the pans in the oven, and immediately reduce the oven temperature to 285 degrees. Bake for 60 to 75 minutes. Do not open the oven door while the pavlovas are cooking.

You'll know the pavlovas are cooked when they look crisp at the edges, which will have started to crack slightly. The top will be dry, but if you press on the underside, it will still be a little soft and squishy. Place the pavlovas back in the oven and leave the door slightly ajar, allowing the pavlovas to cool completely inside.

When they are cool and firm, place one pavlova on a serving platter or cake stand, and spoon a big dollop of whipped cream on top. Scatter a handful of raspberries onto the cream, and then place the second pavlova on top. Again, pile on a good amount of cream and the remainder of the raspberries. Sprinkle with finely chopped chocolate and serve. When you cut into it, you can expect it to crumble and fall apart a bit, but the taste is incredible. No one will care, and it still looks amazing!

Makes 8 to 10 servings.

Ana Cristina's Peanut Buttercream Chocolate Cake

Ana Cristina is the baker in our house. She has studied methods of buttercream preparation and, being quite creative, invented this mouthwatering and sinful recipe.

Chocolate Cake

Cooking spray

1 3/4 cups all-purpose flour, plus
more for dusting the pans

2 teaspoons baking powder

1 teaspoon baking soda

3/4 teaspoon salt

3/4 cup cocoa powder

2 cups pure cane sugar or white sugar

1/2 cup (1 stick) unsalted butter, melted

1 cup whole milk

2 large eggs, room temperature

1 1/2 teaspoons vanilla extract

1 cup very hot water

Peanut Buttercream Frosting

1/2 cup creamy peanut butter

1/3 cup vegetable shortening

1/3 cup salted butter

1 teaspoon vanilla extract

4 cups sifted powdered sugar

5 to 6 tablespoons milk

1 cup mini chocolate peanut butter cups,
half chopped, half left whole

1 (1 1/2-ounce) package peanut butter candy
(like Reese's Pieces)

Preheat the oven to 350 degrees. Coat two 9-inch round baking pans with cooking spray, and dust with flour.

Sift the flour into a large bowl. Add the baking powder, baking soda, salt, and cocoa, and whisk until well mixed.

In a separate bowl, combine the sugar, melted butter, milk, eggs, and vanilla extract. Using an electric mixer on medium speed, beat until creamy. Add the flour mixture one-third at a time, beating well after each addition.

Bring the water to a near boil. Using a wooden spoon, carefully stir the water into the batter until well combined. Pour the batter into the pans.

Place the pans in the oven, and bake the cakes for 30 to 35 minutes, or until a toothpick inserted into the center comes out clean. Place the cakes on a wire rack to cool for 10 minutes. Remove the cakes from the pans, and place them on the rack to cool completely.

To make the frosting, mash the peanut butter, shortening, and butter together in a large bowl. Stir in the vanilla. Using an electric mixer on low speed, gradually add the sugar. Increase the speed to medium-high, and beat well. Gradually add the milk, and beat at medium speed until the desired spreading texture is reached. You may need to add more milk to reach the desired consistency. You want it to be light and fluffy and quite creamy.

Place one cake layer on a serving dish. Frost the top with about one-third of the buttercream, and sprinkle on half of the chopped peanut butter cups. Place the second cake layer on top, and frost the top and sides with the remaining buttercream. Sprinkle the remaining chopped peanut butter cups on the top and a few on the sides. Use the whole peanut butter cups and the candies to decorate the cake.

Refrigerate the cake for at least 1 hour before serving. Serve the cake the day it's prepared. Keep the cake cool to prevent the buttercream from melting. Store leftovers in the refrigerator.

Makes 10 to 12 servings.

ANA CRISTINA CASH'S TIP: Keep buttercream in the refrigerator when it is not in use, and rebeat when ready to use. After frosting and decorating the cake, but before refrigerating it, you can use chocolate shell ice cream topping to make a crisscross pattern around and on top of the cake.

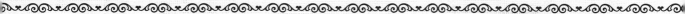

Aunt Fern's Apple Dew Cobbler

My great-uncle's daughter Fern, my mother's first cousin, still lives in Hiltons, Virginia. Her front porch faces north and, on winter mornings, rests under the shadow of Clinch Mountain until nearly ten o'clock in the morning. These cold winter days beg for the warmth of something sweet and comforting, delicious and simple to create. This modern-day version of an apple cobbler makes for tasty eating and is a favorite of Fern's children and grandchildren. Fern wasn't only my mother's cousin; she was her best friend. Mom would fix this delicious treat for her own family as well!

½ cup (1 stick) unsalted butter, softened,
    plus more for greasing the pan

Flour for dusting the pan

4 Granny Smith or other tart green
    apples, peeled, cored, and
    chopped into small pieces

1 cup pure cane sugar or white
    sugar, plus more for topping

½ cup firmly packed dark brown sugar

½ teaspoon ground cinnamon

¼ teaspoon ground cloves

½ teaspoon ground ginger

½ teaspoon vanilla extract

2 (8-ounce) cans refrigerated crescent rolls

1 (12-ounce) can Mountain Dew
    or Mello Yello soft drink

Whipped cream or vanilla ice cream

Preheat the oven to 350 degrees. Butter a 9 x 13-inch baking pan, and dust with flour.

Place the apples, butter, cane sugar, brown sugar, cinnamon, cloves, ginger, and vanilla in a large bowl. Stir with a large spoon until well blended. Remove the crescent dough from the cans, and place the individual pieces in the pan. Top each piece of dough with a heaping tablespoon of the apple mixture.

Fold each piece of dough around the apple mixture, pinch a seam to seal the bundle, and then flip it seam side down in the pan. Pour the soft drink over the bundles, and sprinkle the top with 4 pinches of sugar.

Bake for 45 minutes, or until the sugar begins to caramelize. Remove from the oven, and let cool for 15 minutes before serving with whipped cream or vanilla ice cream. Fern usually serves both!

Makes 8 to 10 servings.

Grand Marnier Bananas Foster with French Vanilla Ice Cream

Bananas Foster is a really easy dish to prepare, with a few precautions. The very nature of the dish is that it is flamed, or set to fire, to burn off the alcohol. It should be very carefully prepared in a well-ventilated area, and please use caution. It may be a good idea to refrain from a sip of the alcohol used in this dessert, as absolute concentration is required. You'll need a long-handled lighter.

1 cup (2 sticks) butter
1 cup firmly packed brown sugar
3 medium ripe bananas, sliced
    into 1/2-inch slices
1 teaspoon vanilla extract
1/2 teaspoon ground cinnamon

1/2 cup banana-flavored liqueur
    (like Bols or DeKuyper)
Long lighter
1/2 cup orange-flavored liqueur
    (like Grand Marnier)
1/2 lemon
2 cups French vanilla ice cream

In a deep skillet melt the butter over medium-low heat, and add the brown sugar. Bring to a boil , stirring constantly, until the sugar is completely melted. Add the bananas, and cook for 3 minutes. Add the vanilla extract and cinnamon. Increase the heat to medium-high, and add the banana liqueur. Immediately light the lighter, and touch the flame to the pan, igniting the alcohol. Continue to stir with a long metal spatula until the flame is completely gone. The heat should not be allowed to get too hot, though boiling should not cease. Add the orange-flavored liqueur, and ignite once more. Stir constantly until the flame dies completely. Turn off the stove, and squeeze the lemon over the banana mixture.

Place a scoop of ice cream in each serving dish, and pour the hot bananas over the top. Serve immediately, as the ice cream melts.

Makes 4 servings.

JOHN CARTER TIP'S: I have found it easier to use a gas stove for this recipe, though an electric stove works; it's just a bit harder to control temperature quickly. It is also important to use a metal skillet (not nonstick) and a long metal spatula.

Honey Butter Broiled Peaches

6 fresh, slightly firm large peaches,
   peeled, halved, and pits removed
Raw or regular honey

4 tablespoons ($\frac{1}{2}$ stick) salted butter,
   cut into 12 equal squares
Pinch of ground cinnamon

Preheat the oven to 375 degrees.

Place the peaches, round side down, on a broiler tray. Drizzle just enough honey in the middle of each peach to fill the small bowl caused by removing the pit. Press a pat of butter into the honey in each peach half. Bake for 10 minutes. Turn the oven to broil. Broil for 3 minutes, or until the butter starts to boil and the peach begins to brown. Immediately remove from the oven, sprinkle cinnamon on top, and serve while still warm.

Makes 6 servings.

Cousin Jack Carter's Tennessee Whiskey Pecan Pie

My cousin, the late Jack Carter, was a one-of-a-kind man. He had a heart the size of Virginia itself, and all who knew him loved him. He lived in Hiltons, Virginia, at the edge of Clinch Mountain, and his home was always a place for festivities. Friends and family from miles around would gather at Jack's and enjoy his generosity and spirit. Jack loved good food, and he did love his Tennessee whiskey. This recipe is in his honor.

1 cup pure cane sugar or white sugar

1 cup firmly packed dark brown sugar

1/2 cup (1 stick) unsalted butter, melted

1 1/2 teaspoons vanilla extract

1/8 teaspoon ground nutmeg

1/8 teaspoon ground cinnamon

4 large eggs

1 1/2 tablespoons Tennessee whiskey

2 cups pecans halves

1 (9-inch) refrigerated piecrust, room temperature

Vanilla ice cream

Preheat the oven to 350 degrees.

In a large bowl combine the cane sugar, brown sugar, butter, vanilla, nutmeg, cinnamon, eggs, and whiskey. Stir until well blended. Stir in the pecans, and pour the mixture into the piecrust.

Bake the pie for 40 minutes, or until the center of the pie has puffed slightly and the top is toasted but not browned too darkly. Let cool just a bit, and serve very warm with a scoop of vanilla ice cream.

Makes 8 servings.

> **JOHN CARTER'S TIP:** To prevent the crust from browning too quickly, lay strips of foil along the crust's rim. Remove the foil during the last 10 minutes of baking.

AnnaBelle Cash's Chess Pie

My daughter AnnaBelle loves adventure, the outdoors, astrophysics, all things space and science, and, of course, good food. Ever since she was a young girl, she has loved the traditional, uniquely Southern dessert chess pie. I have savored many variations of the pie, including chocolate chess, spiced chess, and even grapefruit chess pie. But at our home, we cook only the original, though AnnaBelle likes a little cinnamon sprinkled on top.

1 (9-inch) refrigerated piecrust,
   room temperature
3 tablespoons all-purpose flour
1 tablespoon cornmeal
2 cups pure cane sugar or white sugar
1/4 teaspoon salt
1/2 cup buttermilk, room temperature
1/4 cup whole milk, room temperature

4 large eggs, beaten well, room temperature
1/4 cup (1/2 stick) unsalted butter,
   melted and slightly cooled
1 1/2 teaspoons vanilla extract
Pinch of ground cinnamon or
   cocoa for topping
Whipped cream or vanilla ice cream

Preheat the oven to 350 degrees.

Place the piecrust in the oven for 5 minutes to partially bake. Remove it from the oven, and set aside. Turn the oven up to 450 degrees.

In a large bowl mix the flour, cornmeal, sugar, and salt. In a second large bowl, combine the buttermilk, whole milk, eggs, melted butter, and vanilla, and whisk until creamy. Add the flour mixture to the milk mixture, and stir until well blended. Pour into the piecrust. Place the pie in the oven, and bake for 15 minutes. Reduce the oven temperature to 325 degrees, and bake the pie for another 30 to 35 minutes, until the filling is firm and the top is lightly browned. Remove the pie from the oven, and place it on a wire rack to cool completely. Sprinkle the cinnamon or cocoa liberally and evenly over the top of the pie. Serve with a scoop of whipped cream or a small scoop of vanilla ice cream.

Makes 8 servings.

CHAPTER 7

Late Night Snacks

Bedtime snacks may not be the best choice for digestion, but there are a few late-night treats that help settle the stomach and may lead to more peaceful sleep. Growing up, I often had a decent-size meal just before laying down. I do not recommend this now, but these little tidbits may be suitable at the right time, if appetite demands.

Warm Milk and Local Honey

My children have asked for this bedtime treat since they could talk. It seems to quiet the racing mind and induce a peaceful sleep, as long as you don't consume too much.

1 ½ cups milk
1 tablespoon raw or regular honey

Small shake of ground cinnamon, optional

Place the milk, honey, and cinnamon, if using, in a small pan, and stir well. Heat the milk mixture over medium heat until steaming, stirring often and being sure not to let it boil. Serve hot and enjoy!

Makes 2 servings.

JOHN CARTER'S TIP: A reminder: children under the age of one year should NOT eat honey.

Banana and Cherry Greek Yogurt Smoothie

1 whole banana
1 (8-ounce) container cherry Greek yogurt

½ cup milk
½ cup ice

Place the banana, yogurt, milk, and ice in a blender jar. Blend on medium-high for 3 minutes. Serve while still cold.

Makes 1 serving.

Warm Rice Cereal with Walnuts

2 cups leftover or freshly cooked white rice
1 cup whole milk
1/2 tablespoon salted butter

1/2 teaspoon ground cinnamon
1/4 cup chopped walnuts

Place the rice in a medium saucepan, and add the milk and butter. Heat the rice mixture over medium heat, stirring constantly, until steaming, for about 5 minutes. Add the cinnamon and walnuts, and cook for another few minutes. Serve warm.

Makes 4 servings.

Avocado and Turkey Cottage Cheese Salad

This is the heartiest of my late-night snacks, but turkey contains a natural relaxing chemical and can help induce sleep. Smaller servings are important in the later evening hours, though, as overindulgence can hinder sleep. This recipe is one of my daughter AnnaBelle's all-time favorites.

1 cup chopped leftover or freshly
   roasted turkey breast
½ cup cottage cheese
1 whole avocado, peeled and chopped

1 teaspoon mayonnaise
1 heaping tablespoon finely
   chopped walnuts
Salt and black pepper to taste

In a medium bowl combine the turkey, cottage cheese, avocado, mayonnaise, and walnuts. Stir well. Add salt and black pepper to taste. Refrigerate for at least 1 hour before serving.

Makes 2 servings.

EPILOGUE

This cookbook was never meant to be perfect, not by any stretch. These recipes hold to my family's specific tastes, which may not be your own. I want you to discover your own variations and make things work for your own palate. For example, my family chili is very, very flavorful, much more so than the average American chili, so you may want to use a bit less chili powder and cumin to suit your family's preference. Some dishes are more extravagant, some simple, but each and every one of them is filled with love.

My hope is that this book has connected you with my own family, the diversity of our table, and our willingness to try different foods, even though we retain a distinct flair for Southern cooking at the heart of it all.

May these recipes, along with your own—from whatever passed-down tradition or cookbook—give you a chance to gather closer to the people you love. I believe that around the table, over good food, there's opportunity to connect with perhaps distant children, entwined in video games or their own worlds, and a chance still to learn from our beloved elders. At the table during suppertime, we can be, as much as ever, a family.

John Carter Cash
Hendersonville, Tennessee

ACKNOWLEDGMENTS

Special thanks to:

David Moberg, Kate Etue, Donna Britt, Lou and Karen Robin, Mark Steilper, Cathy Sullivan, Tiffany Dunn, and Trey Call. Tara, Fred, Aran, and Alex Schwoebel. Rosanne Cash, Mary Lauren Teague, Center Point Bar-B-Que, and Café Rakka. Dale, Teresa, and Tucker Jett. The family of Winifred and George T. Kelly, Shane and Ashley Ownby, Loretta Lynn, Patsy Lynn Russell, the Teresita and Rene Alvarez family, the Olga Perez family, and Jane Seymour. Desna, Carl, and all the Jamaican friends. Chuck and Hope Turner. Fern Salyer, Phil and Tammy Salyer, Joey and Jan Salyer, and Shane Salyer. Marty Stuart, Ophelia Jernigan, John Leventhal, Damon Fielder and family, Mike LaMure, Amy Call, Billy Mitchell, Lisa Trice, and Kenan and Sarah McGuffey. The family of Joe Carter, Carlene Carter, Kristin Irving, and Tamara Sovino. The Kristofferson family. The city of Dyess, Arkansas. Thanks to Cindy Cash Panetta, Kathy Cash Tittle. Janene MacIvor, Jenny Baumgartner, Lori Lynch, and everyone else at HarperCollins. Rita Forrester, Adam Clayton, Bono, Larry Mullens Jr., The Edge, Dave Ferguson, Nadine King and all at Maverick Management. A special thank you to the Bisceglea family, Alan Messer, High Garden Woodland Tea House and Sipping Apothecary, Michelle Rollins and family. James, Johnny, and Kris Keach, Tambi Lane, Kim Reynolds, David Tachek, Lauren Moore, David McClister and crew, Jessi Colter, John and Fiona Prine, Annie and Willie Nelson, and the city of Hendersonville, Tennessee.

ABOUT THE AUTHOR

John Carter Cash is a five-time Grammy-winning record producer and author of numerous articles published in popular newspapers and magazines. He owns and manages Cash Cabin Studio. John Carter diligently preserves the family legacy and is the only child of June Carter and Johnny Cash. He lives with his family in Hendersonville, Tennessee.

INDEX